Cuisinart Air Fryer Oven Cookbook for Beginners

1800 Days of Easy Healthy Low-Fat Dining Baking Roasting Frying and Grilling with Expertly Delicious Recipes

Bvangeline Whorne

Table of Contents

INTRODUCTION

Structural Composition of the Cuisinart Air Fryer

The Cuisinart Air Fryer Oven is a versatile kitchen appliance that has gained popularity for its ability to cook food quickly and efficiently using hot air circulation. Understanding its structural composition is essential for optimal use and maintenance

Exterior Design:

The exterior of the Cuisinart Air Fryer Oven is typically made of durable stainless steel or other heat-resistant materials. The sleek design often includes a digital display panel with user-friendly controls, allowing for easy navigation and precise temperature adjustments.

Cooking Chamber:

At the core of the appliance is the cooking chamber, where the magic happens. This chamber is spacious enough to accommodate various types of food, from fries to chicken wings. The interior is usually lined with a non-stick coating to facilitate easy cleaning after use.

Heating Element:

The heating element is a crucial component responsible for generating the

intense heat needed for air frying. Typically located at the top of the appliance, it rapidly heats the air that circulates within the cooking chamber. The element is designed to withstand high temperatures and ensure consistent cooking.

Convection Fan:

Adjacent to the heating element, there is a powerful convection fan. This fan plays a pivotal role in distributing the hot air evenly throughout the cooking chamber. Even air circulation is crucial for achieving that crispy texture associated with air-fried foods.

Temperature and Time Controls:

The digital control panel on the exterior allows users to set the desired cooking temperature and time. This feature provides flexibility, enabling users to tailor the cooking process to different types of food. The temperature control ensures precise cooking, while the timer allows for convenient multitasking in the kitchen.

Cooking Racks and Trays:

To maximize the cooking space and facilitate multi-level cooking, the Cuisinart Air Fryer Oven typically comes with removable racks and trays. These accessories are designed to be easily inserted and removed, providing versatility for cooking various dishes simultaneously.

Drip Tray:

Beneath the cooking chamber, there is a drip tray designed to catch any excess oil or drippings from the food being cooked. This not only makes the appliance easier to clean but also promotes healthier cooking by reducing the overall fat content in the prepared dishes.

Accessories:

Cuisinart often includes additional accessories such as a baking pan, air fryer basket, and skewers. These accessories enhance the versatility of the appliance, allowing users to bake, roast, and even dehydrate in addition to air frying.

Safety Features:

Safety is a priority in the design of the Cuisinart Air Fryer Oven. The appliance is equipped with features like an auto-shutoff function and cool-touch handles to prevent accidental burns. The door is also designed to seal tightly during

cooking, ensuring that hot air is contained within the cooking chamber.

In conclusion, the structural composition of the Cuisinart Air Fryer Oven is a well-thought-out combination of materials and components aimed at providing users with a reliable, efficient, and user-friendly cooking experience. Understanding each part of the appliance allows users to harness its full potential, creating a wide array of delicious and healthier meals. Regular maintenance, including proper cleaning of the components, ensures the longevity and continued optimal performance of this innovative kitchen appliance.

Functions and Benefits

The Cuisinart Air Fryer Oven is a versatile kitchen appliance that combines several functions to streamline cooking and offer a range of benefits for home chefs. Its multifunctionality extends beyond traditional air frying, making it a valuable addition to any kitchen.

Functions:

- Air Frying:

  The primary function of the Cuisinart Air Fryer Oven is, unsurprisingly, air frying. This method of cooking uses hot air circulation to crisp up food, producing a crunchy exterior similar to frying but with significantly less oil. This not only creates healthier versions of traditionally deep-fried favorites but also reduces the overall calorie content of meals.

- Convection Baking:

  The inclusion of convection baking allows the appliance to function as a traditional oven. The convection fan ensures even heat distribution, leading to consistent and efficient baking. This feature is perfect for a wide range of baked goods, from cookies to casseroles.

- Toasting:

  Toasting may seem like a basic function, but the Cuisinart Air Fryer Oven excels in this area. With adjustable temperature controls and multiple

toasting settings, it can cater to different preferences, ensuring your bread, bagels, or pastries are toasted to perfection.

- Broiling:

  The broil function is ideal for achieving a caramelized and slightly charred finish on dishes like meats and vegetables. It's a quick and efficient way to add a delicious crust to your favorite recipes.

- Rotisserie:

  One standout feature is the rotisserie function, allowing you to cook meats like chicken or pork on a rotating spit. This method ensures even cooking and a juicy result, making it a favorite among those who enjoy succulent, rotisserie-style dishes.

- Dehydrating:

  The dehydrating function is perfect for creating homemade dried fruits, beef jerky, or even preserving herbs. It works by circulating warm air at a low temperature, removing moisture and preserving the natural flavors of the food.

Benefits:

- Healthier Cooking:

  One of the primary benefits of the Cuisinart Air Fryer Oven is its ability to cook with significantly less oil compared to traditional frying methods. This makes it an excellent choice for individuals looking to reduce their calorie and fat intake while still enjoying delicious, crispy foods.

- Time Efficiency:

  The convection cooking and air frying features contribute to faster cooking times. The hot air circulation ensures that food is cooked evenly and quickly, making meal preparation more time-efficient, which is particularly valuable for busy households.

- Versatility:

  With multiple cooking functions packed into one appliance, the Cuisinart Air Fryer Oven eliminates the need for multiple kitchen gadgets. It can replace or supplement your toaster, conventional oven, and even your dehydrator, saving both space and money.

- Easy Cleanup:

  Many parts of the Cuisinart Air Fryer Oven are dishwasher safe, making cleanup a breeze. The non-stick interior and removable trays simplify the process, reducing the time and effort required after cooking.

- Energy Efficiency:

  The convection cooking technology not only speeds up the cooking process but also contributes to energy efficiency. The even distribution of heat allows for lower cooking temperatures and shorter cooking times, ultimately saving energy compared to traditional ovens.

In conclusion, the Cuisinart Air Fryer Oven is a versatile kitchen appliance that goes beyond basic air frying. Its multiple functions and associated benefits make it a valuable tool for those seeking convenient, healthy, and efficient cooking options. Whether you're air frying, baking, toasting, broiling, using the rotisserie, or dehydrating, this appliance caters to a wide range of culinary needs, making it a standout in the world of kitchen appliances.

Tips and Tricks for Air Frying Success

Achieving success with your Cuisinart Air Fryer Oven involves mastering various tips and tricks to enhance your cooking experience and produce delicious, crispy results. Here's an extensive guide to help you make the most of your air frying endeavors.

Understanding Your Air Fryer:

Begin by familiarizing yourself with the features and functions of your Cuisinart Air Fryer Oven. Read the user manual thoroughly to comprehend its settings, temperature range, and cooking modes. This foundational knowledge will empower you to make informed decisions while preparing a wide array of dishes.

Preheating Matters:

Preheating your air fryer is a crucial step for optimal results. Just like with traditional ovens, allowing your air fryer to reach the desired temperature before placing food inside ensures even cooking and the development of that coveted crispy texture.

Properly Seasoning Your Food:

Enhance the flavor of your dishes by seasoning them well. Consider marinating meats or coating vegetables with a light layer of oil and your favorite spices. This step not only adds taste but also aids in achieving that golden, crispy exterior.

Use the Right Cooking Oil:

Selecting the appropriate cooking oil is key to achieving the desired crispiness. Opt for oils with high smoke points such as vegetable, canola, or peanut oil. Using a spritzer to apply a thin, even layer of oil on your ingredients promotes a crispy finish without excess grease.

Invest in Cooking Accessories:

Explore accessories designed for air fryers, such as perforated parchment paper or silicone mats. These accessories help prevent sticking and make cleanup a breeze. Additionally, air fryer baskets with multiple layers enable you to cook different foods simultaneously.

Arrange Food Evenly:

For consistent results, arrange food items in a single layer without overcrowding the basket. This allows hot air to circulate freely around each piece, ensuring uniform cooking. If necessary, shake or flip the ingredients halfway through the cooking process.

Monitor Cooking Time:

Keep a close eye on your food, especially during the first few attempts, to avoid overcooking. Air fryers work efficiently and may cook faster than traditional methods. Adjust cooking times based on your preferences and the specific dish you're preparing.

Temperature Control is Key:

Experiment with different temperature settings to find the sweet spot for each type of food. Higher temperatures generally result in a quicker cooking process, while lower temperatures can be ideal for delicate items. It's a balance that often depends on the specific recipe.

Add Moisture When Necessary:

To prevent certain dishes from drying out, consider incorporating moisture. Spritzing a bit of water on foods like chicken or using a water-filled tray in the air

fryer can help maintain juiciness.

Experiment and Have Fun:

Lastly, don't be afraid to experiment with your Cuisinart Air Fryer Oven. Air frying opens up a world of possibilities, from classic favorites to innovative creations. Have fun discovering what works best for you and your taste preferences.

By mastering these tips and tricks, you'll unlock the full potential of your Cuisinart Air Fryer Oven, creating culinary delights with a perfect balance of crispiness and flavor. Happy air frying!

Cleaning And Maintaining

Cleaning and maintaining your Cuisinart Air Fryer Oven is crucial to ensure optimal performance, longevity, and, most importantly, the safety of your cooking. Here's a comprehensive guide to help you keep your appliance in top-notch condition.

Regular Cleaning:

- Exterior Cleaning:

  Wipe down the exterior of the air fryer oven with a damp cloth to remove any grease or food splatters.

  If there are stubborn stains, you can use a mild kitchen cleaner, but avoid abrasive materials that could damage the finish.

- Interior Cleaning:

  Allow the appliance to cool completely before cleaning.

  Remove the cooking racks, trays, and any other removable parts. These are usually dishwasher safe, but check your user manual to be certain.

  Clean the interior with a soft sponge or cloth. If there are any residues, use a mixture of warm water and mild dish soap.

  Be cautious around the heating elements; use a gentle touch to avoid damaging them.

- Drip Tray and Crumb Tray:

  Regularly empty and clean the drip tray and crumb tray to prevent the buildup of grease and food particles. These are usually removable and dishwasher safe for easy cleaning.

Deep Cleaning:

- Remove Residues:

  If there are stubborn residues on the heating elements, use a soft brush or toothbrush to gently scrub them. Do this carefully to avoid damaging the elements.

- Interior Walls:

  Clean the interior walls with a damp cloth or sponge. For any tough stains, you can use a mixture of baking soda and water to form a paste, apply it, and let it sit for a while before wiping it off.

- Air Vents:

  Ensure that air vents are free from obstructions. Use a small, soft brush or a can of compressed air to remove any dust or debris that may accumulate.

Maintaining the Air Fryer Oven:

- Oil and Grease Management:

  Avoid using excessive oil in your cooking to prevent grease buildup.

  Regularly check and clean the air fryer basket and mesh to prevent clogs that could affect air circulation.

- Check Seals and Gaskets:

  Inspect the seals and gaskets for any signs of wear or damage. If you notice any issues, contact the manufacturer for replacement parts.

- Monitor Cooking Times:

  Pay attention to recommended cooking times to prevent overcooking and reduce the likelihood of residues building up.

- Regular Inspections:

  Periodically inspect the power cord for any damage. If you notice any fraying or exposed wires, discontinue use and contact customer service for a replacement.

- Storage:

  Store your air fryer oven in a cool, dry place when not in use. Avoid storing it near heat sources or in areas with high humidity.

Safety Tips:

- Unplug Before Cleaning:

  Always unplug the air fryer oven before cleaning to ensure your safety.

- Follow the Manufacturer's Instructions:

  Refer to the user manual for specific cleaning instructions and any recommendations from the manufacturer.

By incorporating these cleaning and maintenance practices into your routine, you'll not only keep your Cuisinart Air Fryer Oven in pristine condition but also ensure that your culinary creations continue to be a delight. Regular upkeep will extend the life of your appliance and contribute to a safe and enjoyable cooking experience.

Safety Precautions

Safety is of utmost importance when using any kitchen appliance, and the Cuisinart Air Fryer Oven is no exception. Adhering to proper safety precautions ensures a smooth cooking experience and minimizes the risk of accidents. Here are essential safety measures to consider:

Read the User Manual:

Before diving into culinary adventures, thoroughly read the user manual provided by Cuisinart. This document contains crucial information about the appliance's features, operation, and safety guidelines specific to the Air Fryer Oven.

Location Matters:

Place the Air Fryer Oven on a stable, flat surface with sufficient space around it for proper ventilation. Avoid overcrowding the kitchen counter with other appliances, ensuring the Air Fryer Oven has ample room to release heat.

Power Supply:

Connect the appliance to a suitable power source that meets the specified electrical requirements outlined in the user manual. Avoid using extension cords whenever possible.

Proper Ventilation:

Ensure that the ventilation openings on the Air Fryer Oven are not obstructed. Adequate ventilation helps regulate the internal temperature and prevents overheating.

Keep It Clean:

Regular cleaning is not just for hygiene; it's also a safety measure. Grease and food residue can accumulate and become fire hazards. Follow the manufacturer's instructions for cleaning and maintenance.

Unplug When Not in Use:

When the Air Fryer Oven is not in use, unplug it from the electrical outlet. This prevents any accidental activation and reduces the risk of electrical issues.

Avoid Overloading:

Just like any other kitchen appliance, overloading the Air Fryer Oven can lead to uneven cooking and potential safety hazards. Follow the recommended capacity guidelines provided in the user manual.

Check for Damages:

Before each use, inspect the appliance for any damages or signs of wear. If you notice any issues, refrain from using it until the necessary repairs or replacements are made.

Use Proper Accessories:

Stick to the accessories provided by Cuisinart or those recommended in the user manual. Using incompatible or improper accessories can compromise cooking performance and safety.

Caution with Hot Surfaces:

The Air Fryer Oven can become hot during and after operation. Exercise caution when handling the appliance and its accessories, using oven mitts or other protective gear as needed.

1Supervise Children:

Keep children away from the appliance during operation. The Air Fryer Oven involves heat and electrical components, and it's important to prevent accidents by ensuring that young ones are supervised.

1Mindful of Steam:

When opening the appliance, be cautious of the hot steam that may escape. Open the door slowly and away from your face to avoid burns.

1Emergency Procedures:

Familiarize yourself with emergency procedures, such as how to turn off the appliance quickly in case of a malfunction or if you observe any unusual behavior.

By prioritizing these safety precautions, users can enjoy the benefits of the Cuisinart Air Fryer Oven with confidence, knowing that they are taking the necessary steps to create a secure cooking environment. Always prioritize safety to make the most of this versatile kitchen appliance.

Chapter 1: Sauces, Dips, and Dressings

Homemade Salsa Verde Recipe

Prep Time: 10 Mins   Cook Time: 20 Mins   Serves: 2

Ingredients:

- 2 unpeeled garlic cloves
- 1 pound fresh tomatillos husked, washed and stems removed
- 1 onion peeled & quartered
- 2-3 jalapeno chiles or 2 serrano chiles; stems removed
- 3 tablespoons olive oil divided
- ¼ cup chopped fresh cilantro
- ½ -1 teaspoon granulated sugar divided
- ½ cup low-sodium chicken broth
- 1-2 tablespoons fresh lime juice divided
- ½ teaspoon coarse kosher salt
- ¼ teaspoons freshly ground black pepper

Directions:

1. Adjust oven rack to upper-middle position and set oven to broil. Line a large, rimmed baking sheet with aluminum foil.
2. Place garlic, tomatillos, onion, and chilies on the baking sheet and drizzle with 1½ tablespoons olive oil. Set the baking sheet on the oven rack and broil the vegetables until the skins on the tomatillos have darkened and are partially charred.
3. Peel the garlic and scrape all the ingredients (including vegetables, juices & oil) from the baking sheet to a blender.
4. Add cilantro, ½ teaspoon sugar, broth, 1-tablespoon lime juice, ½ teaspoon kosher salt and ¼ teaspoon black pepper. Purée to desired consistency (I prefer the salsa fairly smooth).
5. In a medium saucepan, heat the remaining 1½ tablespoons oil and pour the tomatillo salsa into the pan. Set the heat to medium and bring the salsa to a simmer. Reduce heat to low and cook until mixture reduces to about 2 cups, about 10 minutes. Season to taste with additional sugar, salt, pepper and lime juice, if needed.
6. The salsa is even better when made the day before serving. Keep refrigerated, up to 1 week, in an airtight container.
7. Enjoy!

Nutritional Value (Amount per Serving):

Calories: 338; Fat: 23.67; Carb: 30.43; Protein: 5.89

Oven Roasted Marinara Sauce

Prep Time: 15 Mins   Cook Time: 1 Hr   Serves: 5 cups

Ingredients:

- 4 lbs tomatoes
- 3 large celery stalks
- 1 green bell pepper
- 1 large white onion cut into ⅛th wedges
- 1 small bulb of garlic separate and peel the cloves (more or less to taste)
- 1 ½ teaspoon kosher salt
- ½ teaspoon red chili flakes
- ¼ cup olive oil
- 1 big handful of fresh basil more or less to taste

Directions:

1. Heat the oven to 450°F.
2. Chop the vegetables into large pieces and arrange them in a single layer in a large roasting pan with the garlic cloves. Sprinkle over the salt and chili flakes. Drizzle olive oil over everything, give it a gentle stir, then place the pan in the hot oven.
3. Roast vegetables for approximately 1 hour. The vegetables will reduce and the liquids will bubble. Remove when the vegetables have begun to caramelize (turn deep brown) around the edges. For a thicker sauce, leave in the oven until most of the liquid has cooked away.
4. Allow the vegetables to cool slightly before adding the whole basil leaves and pureeing everything into sauce, either in a standard blender or with an emersion blender in a large heat safe bowl.
5. Use immediately or allow the sauce to cool, and portion in to freezer safe containers to store for up to six months. This sauce can be shelf stable when canned using proper safe canning procedures.

Nutritional Value (Amount per Serving):

Calories: 180; Fat: 12.08; Carb: 15.77; Protein: 5.82

Roasted Marinara Sauce

Prep Time: 15 Mins   Cook Time: 1 Hr   Serves: 6

Ingredients:

- 2 tbsp. olive oil
- 1 onion, chopped
- Kosher salt, to taste
- Freshly ground pepper
- 3 garlic cloves, minced
- 1/4 tsp. red pepper flakes
- 1 tsp. dried oregano

- 28-oz cans peeled whole San Marzano tomatoes (or plum tomatoes)
- 1 lb. spaghetti
- 1/2 c. grated Parmesan cheese
- 1/4 c. basil, thinly sliced

Directions:

1. Heat oven to 350 degrees F.
2. Heat the olive oil in a dutch oven (or a large oven proof pot) over medium heat. Add the onions and season with salt and pepper. Cook for about 5 minutes until translucent. Add the garlic and cook until fragrant, about 30 seconds. Stir in the red pepper flakes and dried oregano and cook for 1 more minute. Using your hands, crush the tomatoes into the pot. Add any remaining liquid. Season with salt and pepper.
3. Cover the pan with a tight-fitting lid and place it in the oven for 1 hour. Let the sauce rest for about 20 minutes before serving.
4. Meanwhile, cook the pasta according to package instructions. Drain and serve with the sauce.

Nutritional Value (Amount per Serving):

Calories: 294; Fat: 6.03; Carb: 55.98; Protein: 8.01

Oven or Air Fryer Easy Pasta Sauce

Prep Time: 5 Mins   Cook Time: 18 Mins   Serves: 4

Ingredients:

- 24oz tomatoes, (the sweetest tomatoes you have), halved or quartered, depending on size.
- 0.17oz dried oregano
- 0.06oz ground allspice, (ground pimento), or to taste.
- 1/3 cup sliced green onions, (spring onions), finely sliced.
- salt
- 0.08oz tsp balsamic vinegar
- 0.17oz tsp maple syrup, use 0.24oz for a sweeter sauce

Directions:

1. Heat your Air Fryer to 350F and get your cake barrel pan ready.
2. Place tomatoes on a cutting board and use a sharp knife to quarter them (If large) or slice in half (if small).
3. Add tomatoes to a mixing bowl and stir in the ground allspice (pimento), dried oregano, and salt.
4. Transfer the tomatoes to the cake barrel pan and place in the heated Air Fryer.
5. Cook for 18 minutes, stirring them a couple of times during roasting.

6. About 3 minutes before cook time ends, add in finely chopped green onions and balsamic vinegar and stir.
7. When done, remove the cake barrel pan from the Air Fryer, let cool, and then blend the sauce to your desired chunkiness/smoothness using an immersion blender. Or you can just mash with a fork.

Nutritional Value (Amount per Serving):

Calories: 37; Fat: 0.44; Carb: 7.78; Protein: 2.17

Air Fryer Campfire Queso Dip

Prep Time: 5 Mins   Cook Time: 10 Mins   Serves: 4

Ingredients:

- 1 pound Taco Meat (ground beef or sausage)
- 8 oz Velveeta Cheese
- 8 oz Montery Jack Cheese
- 15.5 oz can Black Beans (1/2 of the can is all you need)
- 10 oz can of Rotel (1/2 of the can is all you need)
- 4 oz can of Diced Green Chilies (1/2 of the can is all you need)

Directions:

1. Heat your air fryer to 320 degrees.
2. Cube your Velveeta and Montery Jack cheese.
3. In your pan, add your cubed cheeses, cooked taco meat, black beans, rotel, and diced green chilies.
4. Place your pan in your air fryer. Air fry for 10 minutes.
5. Check after 5 minutes, your cheeses should be melting and you can start to stir the ingredients. Continue to air fry for 5 minutes.
6. Give it a good stir and serve immediately with chips.

Nutritional Value (Amount per Serving):

Calories: 948; Fat: 34.96; Carb: 98.42; Protein: 57.78

Air Fryer Spinach Dip

Prep Time: 5 Mins   Cook Time: 40 Mins   Serves 8

Ingredients:

- 8 oz. cream cheese, softened
- 1 cup packed frozen spinach, thawed and water squeezed out
- 1 cup grated parmesan cheese
- 1 cup mayonnaise

- 1/3 cup chopped water chestnuts, drained
- 1/2 cup minced onion
- 1/4 teaspoon garlic powder
- 1 teaspoon black pepper

Directions:

1. Spray the baking vessel with cooking spray or olive oil. Combine all ingredients together (cream cheese, spinach, parmesan, mayo, water chestnuts, onion, garlic powder, & black pepper) in a bowl. Mix to completely combine. Add the dip mixture into the baking vessel(s).
2. Air Fry at 300°F for 20 minutes. After cooking for 20 minutes, stir the dip, and then continue Air Frying at 300°F for 10 minutes.
3. Stir the dip again. Increase heat to 340°F and then continue air frying for 5-10 minutes or until golden brown.
4. If cooking anything less than the full volume of dip, cook for less time and keep checking until it's finished with a brown crust.

Nutritional Value (Amount per Serving):

Calories: 245; Fat: 21.26; Carb: 6.02; Protein: 8.26

Pizza Dip Recipe (Air Fryer)

Prep Time: 10 Mins   Cook Time: 8 Mins   Serves: 6-8

Ingredients:

- 8 ounce package cream cheese, room temperature
- 1/2 cup mayonnaise
- 1/2 cup sour cream
- 2 teaspoons dried Italian seasoning
- 1 teaspoon minced garlic
- 1 teaspoon onion powder
- 1/2 teaspoon salt
- 1/4 teaspoon pepper
- 1 cup shredded mozzarella cheese, divided
- 1 cup Colby Jack cheese, divided
- 25 slices pepperoni
- For dipping
- Corn Chips
- Vegetables, carrots, celery,
- Crackers

Directions:

1. Butter 3 ramekins and set aside.
2. In a large mixing bowl, with a hand mixer, whip the cream cheese until

nice and fluffy, about 1 minute.

3. Add mayonnaise, sour cream and spices (Italian seasoning, minced garlic, onion powder, salt, pepper. Mix until you have a nice and well combine mixture.
4. Add 3/4 cup of shredded mozzarella and 3/4 cup of Colby Jack. Mix until all combined.
5. Evenly divide the mixture into the 3 ramekins.
6. Sprinkle evenly all 3 ramekins with the remaining cheese, ¼ cup of each cheese.
7. Add pepperoni slices on top of the cheese.
8. Air Fry at 400°F for 6 to 8 minutes or until cheese is nice and melted on top.
9. Serve immediately as the cheese will form a crust as it cools off.

Nutritional Value (Amount per Serving):

Calories: 322; Fat: 25; Carb: 9.2; Protein: 15.37

Air Fryer Hot Crab Dip Recipe

Prep Time: 5 Mins   Cook Time: 10 Mins   Serves: 2

Ingredients:

- 8 ounces Cream Cheese - softened
- 1/4 Cup Sour Cream
- 1/4 Cup Mayonnaise
- 1 teaspoon Worcestershire Sauce
- 1/2 teaspoon Old Bay Seasoning
- 2 teaspoons Lemon Juice
- 1 teaspoon Prepared Horseradish
- Pinch Ground Pepper
- 1 Tablespoon Finely Chopped Parsley
- 8 ounces Super Lump Real Crab Meat
- 1/2 Cup Shredded Monterey Jack Cheese – divided

Directions:

1. Mix cream cheese, mayo, sour cream, Worcestershire sauce, Old Bay season, lemon juice, horseradish, pepper and parsley with hand mixer until smooth and fluffy.
2. Fold in crab meat and 1/4 cup shredded cheese.
3. Transfer mixture to a 1 quart oven safe dish.
4. Place dip dish directly into air fryer oven. Air fry at 375°F for 5 minutes.
5. Top with remaining 1/4 cup of shredded cheese.
6. Air fry at 375°F for 4-6 more minutes or until top is browned and bubbly.

Nutritional Value (Amount per Serving):

Calories: 963; Fat: 58.48; Carb: 54.16; Protein: 62.7

Air Fryer French Onion Dip

Prep Time: 10 Mins   Cook Time: 9 Mins   Serves: 4

Ingredients:

- 1 large onion, sliced
- 1/8 cup unsalted butter
- 1 teaspoon garlic salt
- 1 teaspoon thyme
- 1/8 cup beef broth
- 2 ounces room temperature cream cheese
- 1/8 cup sour cream
- 1 1/2 tablespoon mayonnaise
- 1/2 cup shredded mozzarella cheese, divided
- 1 tablespoon grated parmesan cheese

Directions:

1. Start by cutting your onions into thin slices.
2. Then place the butter and cut-up onions into a small skillet. Cook until the onions are caramelized and start to turn golden brown, season with garlic salt and thyme.
3. Mix in the beef broth, and continue to saute everything until most of the beef broth evaporates.
4. Then get out your air fryer safe pan, and toss the onions mixture at the bottom.
5. In a small bowl, mix the cream cheese, sour cream, mayonnaise, 1/4 of a shredded cup, and the Parmesan cheese.
6. Spread that over the onion mixture. Finish it off with the rest of the shredded mozzarella cheese.
7. Set in the air fryer oven and set the time for 9 minutes at 250 degrees F. After the 5 minutes. Check to see if it is bubbling.
8. Plate, serve, and enjoy!

Nutritional Value (Amount per Serving):

Calories: 151; Fat: 11.04; Carb: 6.32; Protein: 7.19

Chapter 2: Breakfast and Brunch

Breakfast Pizza Recipe

Prep Time: 10 Mins   Cook Time: 20 Mins   Serves: 6

Ingredients:

- 8 ounces refrigerated crescent roll dough (1 tube)
- 8 ounces breakfast sausage (Jimmy Dean recommended)
- 1 cup frozen shredded hashbrowns thawed
- 1 cup shredded Mexican cheese blend or your favorite cheese!
- 5 large eggs
- ¼ cup milk
- ½ teaspoon kosher salt
- ½ teaspoon ground black pepper
- 2 tablespoons freshly grated Parmesan cheese

Directions:

1. Heat oven to 375°F. Remove the crescent rolls from the refrigerator and let them come to room temperature for about 15 minutes.
2. Spray a small sheet pan (about 10×15-inches) with nonstick spray. For a deeper-dish pizza, use a 9×13-inch baking dish.
3. Brown the sausage in a skillet and drain.
4. Spread the crescent rolls onto the bottom of the prepared pan. You will have to press and work the dough a little to make sure it covers the pan. Pinch the pieces together.
5. Spoon sausage over the crust.
6. Spread the potatoes over the meat.
7. Sprinkle the cheese over the potatoes.
8. Combine the eggs, milk, salt, pepper, Parmesan together in a separate bowl.
9. Pour the egg mixture evenly over the cheese.
10. Bake in the heated oven for 25-30 minutes, or until the eggs are set. Oven times vary, so check it about halfway through.

Nutritional Value (Amount per Serving):

Calories: 351; Fat: 18.33; Carb: 28.43; Protein: 17.42

Cheesy Sausage and Potatoes Recipe

Prep Time: 10 Mins   Cook Time: 20 Mins   Serves: 8

Ingredients:

- 3 pounds Yukon Gold potatoes peeled and cut into ¼-inch slices
- ¼ cup unsalted butter melted

- 1 pound bulk hot pork sausage
- 1 medium yellow onion chopped
- 2 cups shredded cheese; cheddar Gruyere, Swiss or a mixture
- 2 tablespoons chopped fresh parsley for garnish

Directions:

1. Heat oven to 350°F and spray 13x9-inch baking dish with nonstick cooking spray.
2. Place potatoes in a large saucepan, over medium-high heat, and cover them with cold water. Bring the water to a boil and reduce the heat to low. Cook, uncovered 8-10 minutes or until the potatoes are just fork tender. Drain the potatoes and place them in the prepared baking dish.
3. Pour the melted butter over the potatoes.
4. While the potatoes cook, crumble the sausage in a large skillet set over medium heat. Add the chopped onion and cook until the onion is translucent and the sausage is cooked through. Transfer the sausage/onion mixture to a paper towel-lined plate, and dab the top of the mixture with another paper towel.
5. Spread the sausage/onion mixture over the potatoes and gently toss the mixture together.
6. Top with cheese and bake, uncovered, at 350°F for 7-10 minutes or until the cheese is melted.
7. Garnish with chopped parsley, if desired, and serve.
8. Enjoy!

Nutritional Value (Amount per Serving):

Calories: 499; Fat: 31.8; Carb: 31.88; Protein: 22.24

Air Fryer Tacos

Prep Time: 15 Mins   Cook Time: 4 Mins   Serves: 12

Ingredients:

- 12 Corn Taco Shells Hard Shells
- 1 lb Ground Turkey
- 1 Package Gluten Free or Regular Taco Seasoning
- Shredded Lettuce
- Black Beans Rinsed & Drained
- Shredded Mexican Cheese
- Toppings Tomatoes, Onions, Salsa

Directions:

1. In a medium sized skillet, add the turkey and brown.
2. Drain if needed, add in the taco seasoning as instructed on the package.

3. Build taco with the shell, cooked meat, lettuce, beans, and cheese.
4. Add the tacos to the air fryer. It's best to foil line it and then spray with non-stick cooking spray. Note – Adding foil is optional. If you do foil line the basket of the air fryer, be sure not to fully cover it in order to allow the air to still flow.
5. Cook on 355°F or 360°F for 4 Minutes until crispy. (Some Air Fryers have 355 degrees as an option, and others only have 350 or 360 degrees)

Nutritional Value (Amount per Serving):

Calories: 158; Fat: 8.4; Carb: 10.28; Protein: 10.61

How to Make Scrambled Eggs

Prep Time: 5 Mins   Cook Time: 8 Mins   Serves: 2

Ingredients:

- 4 large eggs
- ¼ teaspoon kosher salt
- ⅛ teaspoon ground black pepper
- 1-2 tablespoons unsalted butter
- Optional Add-Ins
- ¼ cup freshly shredded cheddar cheese
- 1 teaspoon chopped fresh chives
- 2 tablespoons chopped onion
- ¼ cup chopped ham or bacon
- ¼ cup spinach or diced asparagus

Directions:

1. Use a small pan that will fit in the air fryer. Melt the butter in the microwave and pour it into the pan.
2. Whisk the eggs, salt, and pepper together, and pour into the buttered pan.
3. Place the basket into the air fryer and set at 300°F for 4 minutes. Stir the eggs around and set for another 4 minutes. Check for doneness. The eggs are best when they still look wet. They will continue to cook a little even when removed.
4. Stir well and serve immediately.

Nutritional Value (Amount per Serving):

Calories: 231; Fat: 20.4; Carb: 4.53; Protein: 8.57

Air Fryer Fish Tacos Recipe

Prep Time: 10 Mins   Cook Time: 20 Mins   Serves: 12

Ingredients:

- 24 ounces cod filets (about four 6-ounce pieces)
- 4 tablespoons all-purpose flour
- 1 large egg beaten
- 1½ cups Panko breadcrumbs
- 1 teaspoon kosher salt
- 1¼ teaspoons garlic powder
- Olive oil spray
- 12 ounces cabbage mix or coleslaw mix (1 bag)
- 3 ounces Ranch dressing
- 3 tablespoons taco sauce
- 12 corn tortillas
- Optional Toppings
- Lime wedges
- Ranch dressing or sour cream
- Fresh cilantro
- Jalapeño peppers

Directions:

1. Using 3 separate shallow bowls, prepare the fish coating. Place the flour in one bowl and the egg in a second bowl. Place the Panko, salt, and garlic powder in the third bowl and mix to combine.
2. Pat the fish dry with a paper towel. Coat the fish in flour, then egg, then transfer it to the Panko. Bury the fish in Panko and press the crumbs firmly to help them stick to the fish. All sides should be coated with Panko. Repeat with the remaining pieces of fish.
3. Spray or grease the air fryer basket with oil. Place 2-3 pieces in the air fryer, leaving space in between. Spray or dab the tops with oil.
4. Air fry at 375°F for 5 minutes before flipping. Spray or dab with oil, then air fry for another 4-5 minutes. The fish should be golden brown and flake easily with fork.
5. Prepare the coleslaw while the fish is cooking. In a large mixing bowl, combine the cabbage mix, Ranch dressing, and taco sauce. Stir until well combined. Refrigerate until ready to use.
6. Prepare the tortillas on the stove in a skillet set over medium heat. Brown on both sides.
7. Once the fish is done, flake it into large chunks. Prepare the tacos with cabbage mix and fish. Top with lime juice, a drizzle of extra ranch or sour cream, or your favorite toppings.

Nutritional Value (Amount per Serving):

Calories: 300; Fat: 8.47; Carb: 16.39; Protein: 38.47

Air Fryer Breakfast Potatoes

Prep Time: 10 Mins   Cook Time: 25 Mins   Serves: 8

Ingredients:

- 3 Lbs Red Potatoes Diced
- 1/2 Cup Sweet Onion Diced
- 2 Green Bell Peppers Sliced
- 2 Red Bell Peppers Sliced
- 1/2 Tsp Garlic Powder
- 1/2 Tsp Seasoned Salt
- 1/2 Tsp Fennel Seed
- Cooking Oil Spray of Choice

Directions:

1. Begin by preparing the vegetables, and cutting if needed.
2. While preparing, heat the air fryer for 5 minutes at 360°F.
3. Once done, carefully coat a baking sheet with a coat of cooking oil spray such as grapeseed.
4. Add all the vegetables onto the baking sheet.
5. Top evenly with seasonings.
6. Coat with a good coat of cooking oil spray.
7. Cook at 360°F for 20-25 minutes, or until your desired doneness and crispness.
8. It's best to check on there after about 10-15 minutes, to stir or shake up the sheet/pan.
9. Once done, serve.

Nutritional Value (Amount per Serving):

Calories: 114; Fat: 0.3; Carb: 25.91; Protein: 3.28

Air Fryer Biscuits

Prep Time: 8 Mins   Cook Time: 8 Mins   Serves: 8

Ingredients:

- 1 Can Pillsbury Biscuits
- Cooking Oil Spray of Choice

Directions:

1. Coat a baking sheet with cooking oil spray, choices like coconut oil or grapeseed.
2. Evenly place the biscuits on the sheet.
3. Cook at 360°F for 4 minutes.
4. Flip the biscuits and cook an additional 4 minutes at 360°F.
5. Remove and serve.

Nutritional Value (Amount per Serving):

Calories: 19; Fat: 0.25; Carb: 3.77; Protein: 0.51

Air Fryer Cinnamon Rolls

Prep Time: 2 Mins   Cook Time: 8 Mins   Serves: 8

Ingredients:

- 1 Can of Pillsbury Cinnamon Rolls 8-Count
- Coconut Oil Cooking Spray

Directions:

1. Spray the baking sheet/pan of the Air Fryer Oven with Coconut Oil Cooking Spray.
2. Place the cinnamon rolls from the package evenly in the pan/sheet.
3. Set aside the icing.
4. Air Fry the cinnamon rolls for 8 minutes at 360 degrees. (SEE NOTE)
5. Due to the fact that all air fryers heat differently, check in on them around 7 minutes to be sure they are cooking well.
6. Once done, carefully remove and top with icing.
7. Serve.

Nutritional Value (Amount per Serving):

Calories: 18; Fat: 0.65; Carb: 2.95; Protein: 0.24

Air Fryer Breakfast Pizzas with English Muffins

Prep Time: 5 Mins   Cook Time: 5 Mins   Serves: 6

Ingredients:

- 6 Eggs Cooked & Scrambled
- 1 Pound Ground Sausage Cooked
- 1/2 Cup Shredded Colby Jack Cheese
- 3 English Muffins Sliced in Half (6 Halves)
- Olive Oil Spray
- Fennel Seed Optional

Directions:

1. Be sure that both the sausage and eggs are cooked.
2. Spray a cooking sheet/pan of the air fryer oven with olive oil cooking spray.
3. Place each half of muffin in the air fryer oven, typically it will fit 3 and then a second batch to do 3 more.
4. Spray the English muffins with a light coat of olive oil spray, and top them with cooked eggs and cooked sausage.
5. Add cheese to the top of each one, a dash of fennel seed is also a nice addition too, but not required.
6. Cook at 355 degrees for 5 minutes.

7. Carefully remove and repeat for the additional muffins.
8. Serve.

Nutritional Value (Amount per Serving):

Calories: 384; Fat: 23.65; Carb: 14.11; Protein: 28.82

Air Fryer Sausage Patties

Prep Time: 5 Mins   Cook Time: 8 Mins   Serves: 12

Ingredients:

- 1 lb Pork Sausage or Fresh Patties
- Fennel Seed or Preferred Seasoning

Directions:

1. Prepare the sausage by slicing it into patties, or using fresh patties, add fennel seed or any preferred seasoning to the sausage.
2. Heat the air fryer oven at 390°F for about 2 minutes before cooking if preferred.
3. Place evenly in the air fryer oven, and cook at 390°F for 4 minutes.
4. Carefully flip the patties and cook an additional 4 minutes.
5. The internal temperature of the sausage should be at least 160°F to be fully done.
6. Serve.

Nutritional Value (Amount per Serving):

Calories: 125; Fat: 10.37; Carb: 0.79; Protein: 7.08

Chapter 3: Poultry

Tender and Juicy Air Fryer Chicken

Prep Time: 5 Mins   Cook Time: 18 Mins   Serves: 4

Ingredients:

- 2 boneless skinless chicken breasts
- 1 Tablespoons olive oil
- 1 Tablespoon Italian seasoning
- 1 teaspoon garlic powder
- 1/2 teaspoon paprika
- salt and pepper
- optional: brussels sprouts

Directions:

1. Place the chicken in the air fryer basket. Rub olive oil on the chicken.
2. In a small bowl add the Italian seasoning, garlic powder, paprika, salt and pepper. Rub on each side of the chicken.
3. Cook in the air fryer at 360 degrees for 9 minutes. Open the air fryer and flip the chicken. (Add Brussels sprouts now if using). Cook for another 9 minutes or until internal temperature reaches 165 degrees.

Nutritional Value (Amount per Serving):

Calories: 319; Fat: 9.41; Carb: 3.51; Protein: 51.63

Oven Fried Chicken Tenders

Prep Time: 10 Mins   Cook Time: 20 Mins   Serves: 12 chicken tenders

Ingredients:

- 4-5 tablespoons unsalted butter
- 12 boneless skinless chicken tenders or 4 chicken breasts cut into strips
- 2/3 cup flour
- 2 teaspoons sea salt
- 2 teaspoons garlic powder
- 1 teaspoon onion powder
- 1 teaspoon smoked paprika
- 1 teaspoon black pepper
- 2 large eggs
- 2 tablespoons milk
- 1 cup Panko breadcrumbs
- 1/2 cup shredded sweetened coconut (use crushed Cornflakes instead if you are not a fan of coconut)
- 1 teaspoon dried basil

- 1 teaspoon dried parsley

Directions:

1. Heat oven to 400°F.
2. Place butter on a large rimmed baking tray and melt in the oven for a few minutes. Remove baking tray once butter is melted.
3. In a large zip-top freezer bag, combine the flour, salt, garlic powder, onion powder, paprika and pepper. Add the chicken and shake well to coat, pressing through the bag. Set aside.
4. In a shallow bowl, add the eggs and beat lightly with the milk; set aside. In another shallow bowl, combine the coconut, Panko crumbs and dried basil and parsley.
5. Dip each chicken piece in the egg mixture, then coat well into the panko mixture, pressing down to make sure the coating sticks.
6. Place the chicken onto the baking tray. Bake for 12 minutes, using tongs to carefully flip chicken. Bake for another 6-8 minutes (depending on how thick your chicken pieces are). Finish by broiling for 1-2 minutes, or until chicken turns golden and crispy.
7. Remove chicken and pat with paper towels. Enjoy immediately served with your favorite dipping sauce.

Nutritional Value (Amount per Serving):

Calories: 68; Fat: 3.86; Carb: 6.75; Protein: 1.67

Crispy Parmesan Air Fryer Chicken Tenders

Prep Time: 5 Mins   Cook Time: 18 Mins   Serves: 4

Ingredients:

- 1 1/4 pounds boneless skinless chicken tenders
- 1/2 cup white flour
- 1/2 teaspoon salt
- 1/4 teaspoon pepper
- 6 tablespoons olive oil or melted butter
- 3 teaspoons minced garlic
- 1 teaspoon dried basil
- 1/4 teaspoon paprika
- 1 cup Panko breadcrumbs
- 2/3 cup Parmesan cheese, freshly grated

Directions:

1. Trim the fat from the tenders.
2. Set out three bowls. Fill one with white flour, 1/4 teaspoon pepper, & 1/2 teaspoon salt. Stir. Fill the next bowl with olive oil or butter and minced

garlic. Stir. Place the basil, paprika, Panko, and Parmesan cheese in the last bowl. Stir.

3. Place the tenders in the flour mixture, then the garlic oil, then the panko mixture, making sure to evenly and thoroughly coat each piece.
4. Place the tenders in the basket of the air fryer.
5. Cook at 400 degrees Fahrenheit for 9 minutes, flip the tenders, and cook for another 8-9 minutes or until the internal temperature of the chicken reaches 165 degrees Fahrenheit.

Nutritional Value (Amount per Serving):

Calories: 483; Fat: 28.97; Carb: 15.38; Protein: 38.52

Air Fryer Whole Chicken

Prep Time: 5 Mins   Cook Time: 1 Hr   Serves: 8

Ingredients:

- 1 (4-5) pound whole chicken giblets removed
- 2 Tablespoons olive oil
- 1 Tablespoon Italian seasoning
- 1 teaspoon garlic powder
- 1/2 teaspoon paprika
- salt and pepper

Directions:

1. Rub the chicken with the oil. In a small bowl, combine italian seasoning, garlic powder, paprika and salt and pepper. Rub all over the chicken.
2. Place the chicken breast side down in the air fryer. Cook at 360 degrees for 30 minutes.
3. Flip the chicken and cook for an additional 30 minutes or until the chicken reaches an internal temperature of 165 degrees.

Nutritional Value (Amount per Serving):

Calories: 111; Fat: 6.35; Carb: 2.35; Protein: 10.58

Air Fryer Chicken Parmesan

Prep Time: 20 Mins   Cook Time: 13 Mins   Serves: 4

Ingredients:

- 2 Chicken Breasts sliced in half
- 3/4 teaspoon Salt
- 3/4 teaspoon Italian Seasoning Mix

- For the Breading:
- 1/4 cup All Purpose Flour
- 2 large Eggs
- 1/2 teaspoon Garlic Powder
- 1/2 teaspoon Salt
- 1 cup Panko Breadcrumbs
- 1/2 cup grated Parmesan
- For the topping:
- 1 cup Homemade Marinara or Pasta Sauce
- 1 cup shredded Mozzarella
- 1/2 cup grated Parmesan

Directions:

1. Slice each chicken breast in half lengthwise and sprinkle with salt and Italian seasoning mix. Set aside.
2. Create a breading station by placing flour on a plate. In a deep dish, whisk together egg, salt, and garlic powder. Mix panko breadcrumbs and parmesan on another plate.
3. Dust the chicken with flour.
4. Then dip it well into the egg mixture, shake off excess egg.
5. Last coat the chicken in the parmesan panko mixture.
6. Place the chicken on a wire rack and repeat with the remaining chicken.
7. Place in the basket of the air fryer and cook at 390 degrees for 5 minutes. Flip the chicken and cook for an additional 5 minutes. Top with marinara sauce, shredded cheese and cook for an additional 3 minutes in the air fryer until the chicken reaches 165 degrees and cheese is melted.

Nutritional Value (Amount per Serving):

Calories: 211; Fat: 4.4; Carb: 21.21; Protein: 21.15

Air Fryer Honey-Mustard Chicken Thighs

Prep Time: 5 Mins   Cook Time: 15 Mins   Serves: 4

Ingredients:

- 4 boneless skinless chicken thighs
- 1/2 teaspoon onion powder
- 1/2 teaspoon garlic powder
- 1/2 teaspoon smoked paprika
- 1/4 teaspoon salt, or to taste
- 1/4 teaspoon freshly ground black pepper, or to taste
- 2 tablespoons honey
- 2 tablespoons Dijon mustard

- olive oil cooking spray

Directions:

1. Heat the air fryer oven to 390 degrees F, if recommended by the manufacturer. Pat chicken thighs dry with paper towels.
2. For sauce, combine onion powder, garlic powder, smoked paprika, salt, and pepper in a small bowl. Stir in honey and Dijon mustard.
3. Spray one side of chicken thighs with olive oil spray, and place oiled side down in the air fryer in a single layer. Brush the tops of the chicken thighs with the sauce.
4. Air fry at 390 degrees F for 8 minutes.
5. Carefully turn chicken thighs, and brush with remaining sauce. Continue air frying until internal temperature of chicken reaches 165 degrees F, when tested with an instant-read thermometer, 6 to 8 more minutes. Serve warm.

Nutritional Value (Amount per Serving):

Calories: 180; Fat: 3.59; Carb: 9.81; Protein: 26.3

Air Fryer Chicken Tenders

Prep Time: 10 Mins   Cook Time: 12 Mins   Serves: 4

Ingredients:

- cooking spray
- 1 large egg
- 1/2 cup panko bread crumbs
- 2 tablespoons canola oil
- 8 chicken tenders (about 1 lb.)
- chopped fresh parsley, for garnish (optional)
- 2 tablespoons honey mustard sauce

Directions:

1. Heat air fryer oven to 350 degrees F. Coat a baking sheet with cooking spray.
2. Whisk egg in a small bowl. In another bowl, stir together panko and oil until loose and crumbly.
3. Dip each chicken tender into egg, allowing excess to drip off. Dip chicken in panko mixture to coat completely. Working in batches if needed, arrange chicken in an even layer on the baking sheet in the air fryer oven.
4. Cook until chicken is no longer pink in the center and the juices run clear, about 12 minutes. An instant-read thermometer inserted into the center should read at least 165 degrees F. Garnish with parsley and serve with honey-mustard sauce.

Nutritional Value (Amount per Serving):

Calories: 417; Fat: 26.1; Carb: 25.71; Protein: 20.27

Air Fryer Honey Garlic Chicken Wings

Prep Time: 15 Mins   Cook Time: 25 Mins   Serves: 4

Ingredients:

- 1 tablespoon baking powder
- 1 teaspoon salt
- 1/2 teaspoon black pepper
- 1/2 teaspoon garlic powder
- 1/2 teaspoon paprika
- 1/4 teaspoon cayenne pepper
- 2 pounds chicken wings
- 1/2 cup honey
- 1/4 cup soy sauce
- 2 cloves garlic, minced
- 1 tablespoon grated fresh ginger root
- 1 tablespoon cornstarch
- 1 tablespoon water
- 2 tablespoons green onions

Directions:

1. Heat the air fryer oven to 400 degrees F.
2. Mix baking powder, salt, black pepper, garlic powder, paprika, and cayenne pepper together in a small bowl.
3. Pat chicken wings dry with paper towels, then toss them in spice mixture until evenly coated. Arrange wings in a single layer on a baking sheet in the air fryer.
4. Cook wings in the preheated air fryer oven until crispy and golden brown, juices are clear, and meat is no longer pink at the bone, 20 to 25 minutes. An instant-read thermometer inserted near the bone should read 165 degrees F.
5. Meanwhile, make the honey garlic sauce. Stir honey, soy sauce, garlic, and ginger together in a small saucepan over medium heat.
6. In a separate small bowl, whisk together cornstarch and water until smooth, then add to the saucepan. Cook until sauce thickens, 1 to 2 minutes.
7. Transfer wings to a large bowl, pour honey garlic sauce over wings, and toss to coat evenly. Garnish with chopped green onions and serve hot.

Nutritional Value (Amount per Serving):

Calories: 480; Fat: 11.04; Carb: 44.16; Protein: 51.41

Air Fryer Chickpeas

Prep Time: 10 Mins   Cook Time: 15 Mins   Serves: 4

Ingredients:

- 1 (15.5 ounce) can chickpeas, drained and rinsed
- ¾ tablespoon avocado oil
- 2 teaspoons chili-lime seasoning (such as Tajin®)
- ¼ teaspoon garlic powder
- 1 pinch cayenne pepper, or to taste
- salt to taste

Directions:

1. Heat air fryer oven to 400 degrees F. Spray the air fryer basket with cooking spray or use a parchment liner.
2. Place chickpeas on a paper towel-lined plate to dry, patting down with another paper towel on top. Add dried chickpeas to a medium bowl, drizzle with avocado oil, sprinkle with Tajin, garlic powder, and cayenne, and toss to coat.
3. Transfer chickpeas to the air fryer, and cook, stirring or shaking halfway through, until you reach your desired crispness, 12 to 15 minutes. Cooking time may vary depending on the brand and size of your air fryer oven.
4. Season with salt and allow chickpeas to cool slightly.

Nutritional Value (Amount per Serving):

Calories: 117; Fat: 4.22; Carb: 16.02; Protein: 4.74

Air Fryer Ranch Chicken Bites

Prep Time: 10 Mins   Cook Time: 10 Mins   Serves:4

Ingredients:

- 1 pound boneless, skinless chicken thighs, trimmed and cut into 1-inch cubes
- 2 tablespoons avocado oil
- 1 tablespoon white vinegar
- 1 ½ teaspoons dry ranch dressing mix
- 1 teaspoon garlic powder
- ½ teaspoon salt
- ½ teaspoon freshly ground black pepper
- 3 tablespoons shredded extra-sharp Cheddar cheese
- 1 tablespoon chopped fresh parsley

Directions:

1. Combine chicken, avocado oil, white vinegar, ranch powder, garlic powder, salt, and pepper in a large bowl. Stir well until the chicken is coated, cover, and marinate in the fridge for 30 to 60 minutes, but not much longer, as the texture will become mushy.

2. Heat the air fryer oven to 380 degrees F. Place chicken cubes in the air fryer in a single layer, not touching.
3. Air fry until chicken is no longer pink in the center and the juices run clear, flipping once when the edges start to brown, being sure not to overcook, 8 to 11 minutes. An instant-read thermometer inserted near the bone should read 165 degrees F. Your cooking time may vary depending on the brand and size of your air fryer oven, and you may need to cook in batches.
4. Sprinkle the chicken with Cheddar cheese. Return to the air fryer until cheese melts, for about 30 seconds. Serve warm, garnished with chopped parsley.

Nutritional Value (Amount per Serving):

Calories: 304; Fat: 16.99; Carb: 24.62; Protein: 12.7

Air Fryer Frozen Chicken Strips

Prep Time: 5 Mins   Cook Time: 11 Mins   Serves: 8

Ingredients:

- 25 ounces frozen cooked, breaded crispy chicken strips

Directions:

1. Set the air fryer oven temperature to 380 degrees F.
2. Place frozen chicken strips in the air fryer, without touching or overcrowding.
3. Cook until crispy, 11 to 12 minutes. The color will not change much. You may have to cook in batches depending on the size of your air fryer oven, and cooking time may vary depending on the brand and size of your air fryer oven.
4. Remove from the air fryer and serve immediately.

Nutritional Value (Amount per Serving):

Calories: 113; Fat: 3.19; Carb: 19.14; Protein: 2.66

Air Fryer BBQ Chicken Drummies

Prep Time: 5 Mins   Cook Time: 30 Mins   Serves: 4

Ingredients:

- 2 pounds chicken drummies
- 1 ½ tablespoons olive oil
- 1 teaspoon garlic powder
- ½ teaspoon salt

- ⅛ teaspoon freshly ground black pepper
- ¾ cup barbecue sauce

Directions:

1. Heat an air fryer oven to 360 degrees F.
2. Place drummies in a large bowl. Add olive oil, garlic powder, salt, and pepper. Mix until evenly combined. Spread out drummies in the air fryer.
3. Cook drummies for 25 minutes.
4. Using tongs, remove drummies from the air fryer oven and place in a large bowl. Pour barbecue over the top and shake to coat.
5. Place coated drummies back in the air fryer oven. Cook until drummies are no longer pink at the bone and the juices run clear, about 5 more minutes. An instant-read thermometer inserted near the bone should read 165 degrees F. Serve immediately.

Nutritional Value (Amount per Serving):

Calories: 394; Fat: 11.7; Carb: 22.43; Protein: 46.87

Spicy Chicken Jerky in the Air Fryer

Prep Time: 10 Mins   Cook Time: 1 Hr 30 Mins   Serves: 6

Ingredients:

- 2 (5 ounce) boneless chicken breasts, cut into strips
- ½ cup mojo criollo marinade
- 2 teaspoons Cajun seasoning
- 6 wooden skewers

Directions:

1. Combine chicken strips, marinade, and Cajun seasoning in a resealable plastic bag. Refrigerate for 8 hours to overnight.
2. Measure skewers to fit across the air fryer oven, slightly overlapping the edge. Trim off excess length.
3. Heat the air fryer oven to 180 degrees F for 10 minutes.
4. Thread chicken strips onto skewers, leaving room in between each strip, while the air fryer is heating.
5. Air fry for 1 hour 15 minutes. Rearrange the skewers during the reset time.
6. Increase temperature to 200 degrees F and air fry for an additional 15 minutes.
7. Remove strips to a paper towel-lined storage container. Seal. Allow to rest overnight before serving.

Nutritional Value (Amount per Serving):

Calories: 72; Fat: 6.3; Carb: 3.21; Protein: 0.7

Air Fryer Chicken Thighs

Prep Time: 10 Mins   Cook Time: 20 Mins   Serves: 4

Ingredients:

- 4 skin-on, boneless chicken thighs
- 2 teaspoons extra-virgin olive oil
- 1 teaspoon smoked paprika
- ¾ teaspoon garlic powder
- ½ teaspoon salt
- ½ teaspoon ground black pepper

Directions:

1. Heat an air fryer oven to 400 degrees F.
2. Pat chicken thighs dry with a paper towel and brush skins with olive oil. Place chicken thighs, skin-side down, in a single layer on a plate.
3. Combine smoked paprika, garlic powder, salt, and pepper in a bowl. Sprinkle 1/2 of the seasoning mixture evenly over thighs. Turn thighs over and evenly sprinkle with remaining seasoning. Arrange thighs, skin-side up, in a single layer in the air fryer.
4. Cook in the preheated air fryer oven until thighs are brown and the juices run clear, about 18 minutes. An instant-read thermometer inserted into the center should read at least 165 degrees F.

Nutritional Value (Amount per Serving):

Calories: 215; Fat: 11.31; Carb: 1.26; Protein: 27.14

Air Fryer Honey Garlic Chicken

Prep Time: 10 Mins   Cook Time: 25 Mins   Serves: 4

Ingredients:

- 6 Boneless Skinless Chicken Thighs
- Cornstarch or Potato Starch
- 1/2 Cup Honey
- 1/2 Cup Soy Sauce or Gluten Free Soy Sauce
- 2 Tbsp Brown Sugar
- 2 Tbsp Ketchup
- 1 Clove Crushed Garlic
- 1/2 Tsp Ground Ginger
- 1 Tbsp Cornstarch
- Cooked Rice
- Cooked Green Beans

- Sliced Green Onions

Directions:

1. Cut the chicken into cubed chunks, then toss in a bowl with Cornstarch or Potato Starch. Use enough to coat the chicken evenly.
2. Place in the Air Fryer oven and cook according to your Air Fryer Oven Manual for chicken.
3. While the chicken is cooking, in a small saucepan, combine the honey, soy sauce, brown sugar, ketchup, garlic, and ginger.
4. Bring this to a low boil, then whisk in the cornstarch until the sauce is thickened.
5. Set aside.
6. Once the chicken is cooked, mix it into the sauce and warm up. This can be done in a small skillet or the saucepan, simply coat the chicken with the sauce. It will be a sticky texture sauce.
7. Serve the chicken over cooked rice with green beans.
8. Garnish with green onion.

Nutritional Value (Amount per Serving):

Calories: 508; Fat: 5.7; Carb: 64.73; Protein: 50.14

Chicken Pesto (Air Crisp)

Prep Time: 2 Mins   Cook Time: 18 Mins   Serves: 4

Ingredients:

- 1/2 Cup Basil Pesto Sauce
- 4 Boneless, Skinless Chicken Thighs
- Fresh Mozzarella (Optional)
- Sliced Roma Tomatoes (Optional)
- Grapeseed Oil Spray

Directions:

1. Coat a baking sheet with grapeseed oil spray.
2. Add the pesto to a bowl, then coat each chicken thigh well with the pesto.
3. Place the baking sheetinto the Air Fryer Oven, then evenly add the chicken.
4. Use the Air Fry function at 390°F for 15-18 minutes, check-in on the chicken halfway through the cooking time to make sure it does not overcook. Flip the chicken if needed. The internal temperature should be 165°F to be fully cooked.
5. Once the chicken is cooked, if preferred, carefully top it with fresh mozzarella and heat for an additional 2 minutes to melt the mozzarella.
6. Serve topped with sliced Roma tomatoes.

Nutritional Value (Amount per Serving):

Calories: 361; Fat: 23.83; Carb: 22.54; Protein: 14.71

Air Fried Turkey

Prep Time: 10 Mins   Cook Time: 1 Hr   Serves: 6

Ingredients:

- 3 Lb Butterball Turkey Roast White & Dark Meat
- 2 Tbsp Olive Oil
- 1/2 Tsp Dried Rosemary
- 1 Tsp Dried Parsley
- 1/2 Tsp Garlic Salt

Directions:

1. In a small bowl combine the seasonings with the olive oil.
2. Cut the netting carefully off the roast, and be very careful with it to keep it all together.
3. Turn the air fryer oven to air fry at 350°F for 5 minutes to warm it up.
4. Coat a baking sheet with olive oil cooking spray.
5. Place the roast in the air fryer.
6. Using a brush, completely coat the roast with the olive oil mixture.
7. Cook in the air fryer oven at 350°F for 20 minutes.
8. Open the door and coat the turkey with another coat of olive oil spray if needed.
9. Continue cooking for an additional 30 minutes or until the internal temperature reaches at least 165°F. This could mean a few extra minutes depending on how hot the air fryer oven you use gets.
10. Once done, carefully remove and plate to serve.

Nutritional Value (Amount per Serving):

Calories: 285; Fat: 10.18; Carb: 0.33; Protein: 48.29

Chapter 4: Beef, Pork and Lamb

Air Fryer Steak

Prep Time: 10 Mins   Cook Time: 20 Mins   Serves: 2 steaks

Ingredients:

- 1-2 Ribeye New York, or Tri Tip Steaks (1 inch thick)
- 1 tablespoon olive oil
- 1 teaspoon Italian seasoning
- salt and pepper
- Garlic Herb Butter:
- 1/4 cup butter softened
- 1 garlic clove minced
- 1 teaspoon fresh rosemary
- 1 teaspoon fresh thyme
- 1 teaspoon fresh parsley

Directions:

1. Heat the air fryer to 400 degrees. Prepare the steaks by rubbing olive oil on each side. Rub the Italian seasoning, and salt and pepper on each side.
2. Add the steak to the air fryer basket and cook for 12 minutes, turning over after 6 minutes for medium. Let the steak rest for 10 minutes and top with garlic butter.

Nutritional Value (Amount per Serving):

Calories: 1182; Fat: 81.54; Carb: 3.8; Protein: 102.75

Air Fryer Pork Fajitas Recipe

Prep Time: 10 Mins   Cook Time: 12 Mins   Serves: 4

Ingredients:

- 1 Pound Pork Tenderloin, sliced thin
- 2 tablespoons Olive Oil
- 3 tablespoons Fajita Seasoning
- 1 1/2 cups Bell Peppers, any color combination (sliced)
- 1/2 cup Purple Onion, sliced
- Flour Tortillas (for serving)

Directions:

1. Pat the tenderloin with a paper towel, and cut it into thin slices. This will help it cook evenly. Add it to a medium-sized bowl with bell peppers and onion.
2. Add in the olive oil and fajita seasoning, and toss to coat.
3. Add it to the basket of your air fryer. Cook at 390 degrees for 12 minutes

or until cooked throughout and no longer pink. Serve with homemade tortillas if desired.

Nutritional Value (Amount per Serving):

Calories: 246; Fat: 10.41; Carb: 12.68; Protein: 23.5

Air Fryer Beef Tenderloin Recipe

Prep Time: 10 Mins   Cook Time: 20 Mins   Serves: 6

Ingredients:

- 3 pounds beef tenderloin trimmed and tied (see note)
- 4 tablespoons unsalted butter room temperature (½ stick)
- 2 cloves garlic grated
- 1 teaspoon minced fresh rosemary
- 1 teaspoon kosher salt
- ½ teaspoon freshly ground black pepper
- ½ teaspoon minced fresh thyme
- ½ teaspoon minced fresh sage

Directions:

1. Bring the beef tenderloin to room temperature by allowing it to sit on the counter for at least 30 minutes before cooking.
2. In a small bowl, stir the softened butter, grated garlic, rosemary, salt, pepper, thyme, and sage together.
3. Pat the beef tenderloin dry with a paper towel and then rub the compound butter evenly over every side.
4. Place the beef tenderloin in the air fryer and cook it at 400°F for 5 minutes.
5. Reduce the heat to 350°F and continue to cook the tenderloin for another 12-15 minutes, or until the internal temperature of the beef reaches 120°F with an instant read thermometer.
6. Cover the beef tenderloin with foil and allow it to rest for 10 minutes before slicing.
7. Serve the beef tenderloin with your favorite sides and enjoy immediately.

Nutritional Value (Amount per Serving):

Calories: 551; Fat: 28.08; Carb: 0.42; Protein: 69.55

Air Fryer Beef and Broccoli Recipe

Prep Time: 40 Mins   Cook Time: 15 Mins   Serves: 4

Ingredients:

- ⅓ cup soy sauce

- ¼ cup water
- 2 tablespoons sesame oil
- 3 cloves garlic minced
- 1 teaspoon grated ginger
- 1 teaspoon sriracha optional
- 1 pound flank steak thinly sliced
- 1 pound broccoli florets
- 1 teaspoon olive oil
- ½ teaspoon cornstarch
- Cooked rice for serving
- Sesame seeds and sliced green onion for garnish

Directions:

1. In a small mixing bowl, combine the soy sauce, water, sesame oil, garlic, ginger, and sriracha.
2. Place the sliced steak in a shallow bowl and pour half of the sauce over it. Reserve the other half of the sauce for later. Cover the bowl and let the steak marinate in the refrigerator for 30 minutes.
3. Place the marinated steak into the air fryer basket and cook at 375°F for 8 minutes.
4. Toss the broccoli and olive oil together, and add it to the basket (on top of the steak). Cook at 375°F for an additional 4 minutes.
5. Add the cornstarch to the reserved sauce and microwave it for 1 minute. Whisk to combine and microwave for an additional minute. The sauce should have thickened enough to coat the back of a spoon – if it is too thick, add a splash of water. If it is too thin, cook it for an additional minute.
6. Pour the finished sauce over the cooked beef and broccoli. Serve with rice and garnish with sesame seeds and sliced green onion, if desired.

Nutritional Value (Amount per Serving):

Calories: 528; Fat: 44.22; Carb: 10.51; Protein: 24.39

Air Fryer Pork Chops Recipe

Prep Time: 10 Mins   Cook Time: 10 Mins   Serves: 2

Ingredients:

- 4 boneless pork chops
- 2 tablespoons olive oil
- 1 teaspoon kosher salt
- ½ teaspoon ground black pepper
- 1 teaspoon onion powder
- 1 teaspoon garlic powder
- 1 teaspoon smoked paprika
- ½ teaspoon ground mustard
- ½ cup Parmesan cheese finely grated

Directions:

1. Heat air fryer to 375°F for 5 minutes.
2. Brush the pork chops with olive oil. Set aside.
3. In a shallow bowl, combine the salt, pepper, onion powder, garlic powder, paprika, mustard, and Parmesan cheese.
4. Press both sides of each pork chop into the Parmesan coating.
5. Spray the inner basket with nonstick spray. Place the pork chops in a single layer in the basket.
6. Cook for 4 minutes. Flip the pork chops and cook for another 3-5 minutes, or until the internal temperature reaches 145°F. Remove the pork chops from the air fryer and serve.

Nutritional Value (Amount per Serving):

Calories: 683; Fat: 27.53; Carb: 11.9; Protein: 91.82

Country Style Ribs (Air Fryer)

Prep Time: 5 Mins   Cook Time: 20 Mins   Serves: 4

Ingredients:

- 2 Pounds Boneless Country Style Pork Ribs
- Head Country Seasoning
- Barbecue Sauce

Directions:

1. Heat the air fryer oven to 375°F for about 5 minutes.
2. While this is heating, coat the ribs with seasoning and sauce.
3. Once coated well, spray a baking sheet with cooking spray of your choice.
4. Add the ribs to the air fryer oven and cook at 375°F for 20 minutes, flipping them after 10 minutes.
5. Cook until the internal temperature reaches at least 145°F or to your desired doneness.

Nutritional Value (Amount per Serving):

Calories: 152; Fat: 5.58; Carb: 2.98; Protein: 20.58

Ham Recipe

Prep Time: 5 Mins   Cook Time: 30 Mins   Serves: 6

Ingredients:

- 3 lb Boneless Cooked Ham
- 3 Tbsp Brown Sugar
- Olive Oil Spray
- Parsley

- Glaze Optional

Directions:

1. Coat a baking sheet with olive oil cooking spray.
2. Place the ham on the sheet, you can also use aluminum foil and place it on it to avoid a messy basket if using the glaze.
3. Once the ham is in the oven, coat with brown sugar and top evenly with parsley and a coat of olive oil cooking spray.
4. Cook using the air fryer function at 350°F for 30 minutes.
5. If you are using the glaze, prepare the glaze while the ham is in the air fryer, and add it in the last 5-10 minutes of cook time. Just carefully coat the ham with it and then finish cooking.

Nutritional Value (Amount per Serving):

Calories: 439; Fat: 18.75; Carb: 8.55; Protein: 59.59

Beef Roast

Prep Time: 15 Mins   Cook Time: 1 Hr   Serves: 6

Ingredients:

- 3 Lb Beef Chuck Roast
- 1 Tsp Steak Seasoning
- 1 Package Gluten-Free or Regular Brown Gravy Mix
- 1/2 Cup Water
- 4 Tbsp Unsalted Butter
- Parsley or Rosemary to Garnish

Directions:

1. Begin by heating the air fryer oven to 390°F for 5 minutes.
2. While this is heating, season the roast evenly with steak seasoning.
3. Combine the gravy with 1/2 cup water and set aside.
4. Once the heating time is up, carefully spray a baking pan with grapeseed cooking oil spray.
5. Place the roast into the fryer oven and cook it on air fry at 390°F for 15 minutes, searing the outside.
6. Once the cooking time is up, prepare a sheet of foil to place the roast on.
7. Carefully remove the roast from the fryer oven and place it on the foil.
8. Roll up the foil around the sides of the roast and place it back into the oven.
9. At this point, be sure the foil is up around the sides so the air can circulate.
10. Carefully pour the brown gravy mixture over the roast.
11. Place the butter on top of the roast.
12. Cook on air fry for 30-40 minutes at 325°F, the internal temperature

needs to reach at least 145°F.

13. Once done, let it rest for 5 minutes and then slice and serve.
14. Roast can be served with drippings as gravy.

Nutritional Value (Amount per Serving):

Calories: 647; Fat: 32.7; Carb: 3.98; Protein: 84.32

Tri Tip

Prep Time: 5 Mins   Cook Time: 15 Mins   Serves: 4

Ingredients:

- 1 1/2 – 2 LB Tri Tip Cut
- 1 Tbsp Steak Seasoning
- Cooking Oil Spray of Choice Grapeseed, Etc.

Directions:

1. Season the steak with the steak seasoning and let rest for about 15 minutes before cooking.
2. Coat a baking sheet with the spray of your choice such as grapeseed.
3. Once ready to cook, place in the fryer oven and use the Air Fry setting at 400°F for 15 minutes, rotate the steak about halfway through the cooking time.
4. Carefully remove, slice against the grain and serve.
5. It's best to watch this steak closely as you want it to reach an internal temperature of about 145°F. This is the sweet spot for this steak, less on the temperature if you are looking for it to be rarer.

Nutritional Value (Amount per Serving):

Calories: 8; Fat: 0.06; Carb: 1.26; Protein: 0.1

Air Fryer Beef Fajitas

Prep Time: 5 Mins   Cook Time: 15 Mins   Serves: 12

Ingredients:

- 1 Pound Certified Angus Beef Skirt Steak or Flank Steak
- 1 Red Bell Pepper Diced
- 1 Green Bell Pepper Diced
- 1 Yellow Bell Pepper Diced
- 1 Orange Bell Pepper Diced
- 1/4 Cup Sweet Onion Diced
- 4 Tbsp Fajita Seasoning or 1 Packet

- Corn or Flour Tortillas

Directions:

1. Start by cutting the steak against the grain.
2. Spray a baking pan with olive oil cooking spray, and place the steak in the air fryer oven.
3. Top with the vegetables and the seasoning evenly.
4. Spray with another coat of olive oil cooking spray.
5. Cook at 390 degrees for 5 minutes.
6. Open the air fryer oven and mix up the ingredients, being sure everything is well coated with seasoning, and add an additional spray of olive oil cooking spray.
7. Cover and cook using the air fryer function for an additional 5-10 minutes at 390 degrees to your desired doneness. (We find that cooking for another 7 minutes is a perfect time, after 5 minutes, open it and check to see if it's to your desired doneness, if not add an additional 2-5 minutes.)
8. Serve on warm tortillas.

Nutritional Value (Amount per Serving):

Calories: 122; Fat: 3.4; Carb: 18.12; Protein: 4.72

Steak Wrapped Asparagus (Air Fryer)

Prep Time: 10 Mins   Cook Time: 10 Mins   Serves: 6

Ingredients:

- 1 Pound Asparagus Trimmed
- 2 Cups Grape Tomatoes Halved
- 1 1/2 Pound Skirt Steak or Flank Steak Thinly Sliced
- 4 Tbsp Balsamic Vinegar
- 4 Tbsp Olive Oil
- 1 Clove Garlic Crushed
- 1 Tsp Salt
- Olive Oil Cooking Spray

Directions:

1. Spray a baking sheet lightly with olive oil spray.
2. Slice the steak against the grain into 6 pieces, as evenly as possible.
3. In a small bowl, combine the vinegar, oil, garlic, and salt. Just lightly mix it. It's not going to fully combine.
4. Take about 3 asparagus and place them in 1 slice of steak, roll it up and place it in the fryer oven.
5. Continue this process for all of the steak.
6. Once there are 3 in the fryer oven, add in half of the tomatoes.

7. Using a brush, brush the steaks and the vegetables with the oil and vinegar mixture.
8. Cook using the air fry function at 390 degrees for 10 minutes using the attached lid. (Note - I do recommend checking on them at 5 minutes, we prefer them cooked until 10 minutes, but your desired doneness may vary.)
9. Carefully remove and repeat the process for the remaining 3 steaks.
10. Serve the steak wrapped asparagus with tomatoes.

Nutritional Value (Amount per Serving):

Calories: 183; Fat: 12.99; Carb: 14.04; Protein: 4.42

Bacon Wrapped Jalapeño Poppers (Air Fryer)

Prep Time: 10 Mins   Cook Time: 15 Mins   Serves: 10

Ingredients:

- 5 Jalapeño Peppers Halved to make 10
- 4 oz Cream Cheese
- 1/2 Tsp Garlic Salt
- 10 Slices of Thick Cut Bacon
- 10 Little Sausages

Directions:

1. Start by halving the peppers if not already, be sure to wear gloves while making these as they can make your hands burn depending on the heat of the peppers.
2. In a small bowl combine the cream cheese and garlic salt.
3. Take half the pepper and add a bit of cream cheese to it.
4. Add one sausage on top of the cream cheese.
5. Wrap one slice of bacon around the pepper and sausage, be sure the start of the bacon is on the bottom, and then finish it on the bottom, so that when it sits in the air crisp basket, it does not come undone.
6. Place each one in the air fryer oven.
7. Cook for 10 minutes at 375 degrees.
8. Check in on them at 10 minutes, add an additional 5 minutes if needed.
9. Thick cut bacon typically takes a total of 15 minutes; however, thin cut takes about 10 minutes. By starting at 10 minutes and adding an additional 5 minutes, this will help you avoid overcooking, and check in on the peppers first.

Nutritional Value (Amount per Serving):

Calories: 277; Fat: 22.58; Carb: 7.71; Protein: 13.79

Air Fryer Beef Fried Rice

Prep Time: 10 Mins   Cook Time: 20 Mins   Serves: 6

Ingredients:

- 1/2 Pound Skirt Steak sliced against the grain
- 4 Cups Cold Cooked White Rice
- 1/4 Cup White Onion Diced
- 1/4 Cup Celery Diced
- 1/4 Cup Carrots Diced
- 4-6 Tbsp Soy Sauce or Gluten Free Soy Sauce
- Coconut Oil Cooking Spray or Olive Oil Cooking Spray
- 2 Great Day Farms Hard-Boiled Eggs

Directions:

1. Cut the steak and place it in the air fryer oven.
2. Cook at 390 degrees for 5 minutes.
3. Turn and cook an additional 5 minutes.
4. Line a baking pan with foil.
5. Spray the foil with the coconut oil or olive oil spray.
6. Add all ingredients in order on top of the foil in the oven.
7. Stir to mix together and add a nice coat of coconut oil spray to the top of the mixture.
8. Cook in the air fryer oven on 390°F for 5 minutes.
9. Carefully open and stir up the rice and mixture again, adding an additional coat of spray or soy sauce if needed.
10. Stir in the sliced or crumbled hard-boiled eggs.
11. Continue cooking for an additional 3 minutes at 390°F.
12. Stir up and serve.

Nutritional Value (Amount per Serving):

Calories: 382; Fat: 23.2; Carb: 43.13; Protein: 23.99

Air Fryer Ranch Breaded Pork Chops

Prep Time: 5 Mins   Cook Time: 8 Mins   Serves: 4

Ingredients:

- 4 Boneless Thin Pork Chops (1/4 inch thick)
- 2 Beaten Eggs
- 1 Package Ranch Seasoning Mix
- 1/4 Cup Bread Crumbs or Gluten-Free Bread Crumbs

Directions:

1. Place the beaten eggs in one bowl.
2. In a separate bowl, mix together the seasoning mix and bread crumbs.
3. Dip the pork chops in the eggs, shake off the excess.

4. Dip in the seasoning mixture and then place in the sprayed air fryer oven. It's best to spray a baking pan with non-stick cooking spray or to line it with foil and spray the foil.
5. Cook at 360 degrees for 4 minutes.
6. Carefully turn the pork chops and cook for an additional 4 minutes. At this point, if you prefer, lightly spray them with cooking oil such as olive oil. Pork Chops should be at 145 degrees to be fully cooked.
7. Serve.

Nutritional Value (Amount per Serving):

Calories: 671; Fat: 11.22; Carb: 67.37; Protein: 51.24

Air Fryer Bacon

Cook Time: 10 Mins   Total Time: 10 Mins   Serves: 4

Ingredients:

- 1 Pound Bacon

Directions:

1. Add bacon into the air fryer oven on a baking sheet, evenly. This may take 2 batches to cook all of the bacon, depending on size.
2. Cook at 350 degrees for 5 minutes.
3. Turn bacon and cook an additional 5 minutes or until your desired crispiness.
4. Remove bacon with tongs and place on a paper towel lined plate.
5. Let cool and serve.

Nutritional Value (Amount per Serving):

Calories: 352; Fat: 33.48; Carb: 7.17; Protein: 12.11

Air Fryer Korean BBQ Beef

Prep Time: 15 Mins   Cook Time: 30 Mins   Serves: 4

Ingredients:

- MEAT
- 1 Pound Flank Steak or Thinly Sliced Steak
- 1/4 Cup Corn Starch
- Pompeian Oils Coconut Spray
- SAUCE
- 1/2 Cup Soy Sauce
- 1/2 Cup Brown Sugar
- 2 Tbsp Pompeian White Wine Vinegar

- 1 Clove Garlic Crushed
- 1 Tbsp Hot Chili Sauce
- 1 Tsp Ground Ginger
- 1/2 Tsp Sesame Seeds
- 1 Tbsp Cornstarch
- 1 Tbsp Water

Directions:

1. Begin by preparing the steak. Thinly slice it then toss in the cornstarch.
2. Spray a baking sheet or line it with foil in the air fryer oven with coconut oil spray.
3. Add the steak and spray another coat of spray on top.
4. Cook in the air fryer oven for 10 minutes at 390°F, turn the steak and cook for an additional 10 minutes.
5. While the steak is cooking, add the sauce ingredients EXCEPT the cornstarch and water to a medium saucepan.
6. Warm it up to a low boil, then whisk in the cornstarch and water.
7. Carefully remove steak and pour sauce over the steak, mix well.
8. Serve topped with sliced green onions, cooked rice, and green beans.

Nutritional Value (Amount per Serving):

Calories: 356; Fat: 17.4; Carb: 45.26; Protein: 5.79

Air Fryer Bacon Wrapped Corn on the Cob

Prep Time: 5 Mins   Cook Time: 20 Mins   Serves: 4

Ingredients:

- 4 Trimmed Corn on the Cob
- 8 Slices of Bacon

Directions:

1. Place foil on a baking sheet in the air fryer oven.
2. Wrap the bacon around each corn on the cob.
3. Place in the air fryer oven.
4. Cook at 355°F for 10 minutes on each side or until crispy.
5. Serve.

Nutritional Value (Amount per Serving):

Calories: 261; Fat: 20.81; Carb: 12.18; Protein: 8.16

Air Fryer Glazed Steaks

Prep Time: 4 Hrs   Cook Time: 20 Mins   Serves: 2

Ingredients:

- 2 Sirloin Steaks at least 6oz
- 2 Tbsp Soy Sauce
- 1/2 Tbsp Worcestershire Sauce
- 2 Tbsp Brown Sugar
- 1 Tbsp Grated Peeled Ginger
- 1 Tbsp Garlic Crushed
- 1 Tsp Seasoned Salt
- Salt/Pepper to Taste

Directions:

1. In a large seal-able bag, add the steaks along with the remaining ingredients.
2. Seal it up and let it marinate in the fridge for at least 8 hours.
3. Place foil on a baking pan in the air fryer oven, spray with non-stick cooking spray, and then place steaks on it.
4. Cook steaks at 400°F for 10 minutes.
5. Rotate steaks and cook an additional 10-15 minutes or until your desired doneness.

Nutritional Value (Amount per Serving):

Calories: 1237; Fat: 69.08; Carb: 21.12; Protein: 124.76

Perfect air fryer steak: paleo, whole30, keto, easy!

Prep Time: 5 Mins   Cook Time: 12 Mins   Serves: 2

Ingredients:

- 2 sirloin steaks
- 2–3 tbsp steak seasoning
- Spray oil or cooking fat of choice (I prefer avocado oil)

Directions:

1. First, pat the steak dry and let come to room temperature.
2. Spray (or brush) oil lightly on the steak and season liberally.
3. Spray or coat a baking sheet of the air fryer oven with oil, and place the steaks into the air fryer oven. The steaks can be touching or sort of "smooshed" in the oven.
4. Cook on 400 degrees F. for 6 minutes, flip the steaks and cook for another 6 minutes. If you want your steak more well-done, add an additional 2-3 minutes. Let rest before serving.

Nutritional Value (Amount per Serving):

Calories: 1151; Fat: 66.23; Carb: 4.99; Protein: 123.22

Chapter 5: Fish and Seafood

Air Fryer Frozen Shrimp

Prep Time: 8 Mins   Cook Time: 8 Mins   Serves: 4

Ingredients:

- 16 ounces breaded frozen shrimp
- non-stick cooking spray
- squeeze of lemon, optional

Directions:

1. Heat the air fryer to 400 degrees Fahrenheit.
2. Add the frozen shrimp to the air fryer tray or basket in a single layer. Spray with non-stick cooking spray if you want it crispy.
3. Close the basket and cook in the air fryer for 8 minutes, flipping the shrimp halfway through at the 4-minute mark.

Nutritional Value (Amount per Serving):

Calories: 119; Fat: 2.88; Carb: 14.68; Protein: 8.8

Air Fryer Lobster Tails

Prep Time: 15 Mins   Cook Time: 10 Mins   Serves: 4 lobsters

Ingredients:

- 4 lobster tails
- salt and pepper
- 1/4 cup butter melted
- 3 garlic cloves minced
- 1/2 teaspoon paprika
- 1 teaspoon parsley chopped

Directions:

1. Start by preparing the lobster. Using kitchen shears butterfly the tail by cutting down the center. Loosen the meat and pull the lobster meat upward. Salt and pepper the meat and set it on a baking sheet.
2. In a small bowl, whisk together the melted butter, garlic, paprika, thyme, rosemary, and parsley. Spread evenly on each lobster tail.
3. Place the lobster tail in the basket of the air fryer. Cook at 380 degrees for 5-7 minutes or until the meat is opaque and lightly brown. Serve with melted butter.

Nutritional Value (Amount per Serving):

Calories: 226; Fat: 12.73; Carb: 2.05; Protein: 25.26

Insanely Delicious Air Fryer Coconut Shrimp

Prep Time: 5 Mins   Cook Time: 10 Mins   Serves: 4

Ingredients:

- 1 pound large shrimp about 25, peeled (tails left on), deveined
- 2 large eggs
- 1 cup flaked unsweetened coconut
- 1/2 cup panko breadcrumbs
- 1/2 cup all-purpose flour
- 1/2 teaspoon garlic powder
- 1/2 teaspoon paprika optional
- Salt and freshly ground black pepper

Directions:

1. Beat eggs in a small bowl and set aside. Combine breadcrumbs and coconut in another bowl and set aside. Lastly, combine flour and spices in a 3rd bowl.
2. Dip shrimp in small batches in the flour mixture, then the egg mixture (letting the excess drip off the shrimp), and then coat in the coconut/breadcrumb mixture, pressing to adhere.
3. Place the shrimp in the basket of the air fryer. Cook at 360 degrees for 10 minutes, flipping half way through or until shrimp is cooked throughout.

Nutritional Value (Amount per Serving):

Calories: 119; Fat: 3.27; Carb: 17.36; Protein: 4.81

Air Fryer Fish Sticks

Prep Time: 10 Mins   Cook Time: 15 Mins   Serves: 4

Ingredients:

- 1 pound cod sliced into strips
- salt and pepper
- 1/2 cup flour
- 2 large eggs
- 1/2 teaspoon salt
- 1 cup Panko
- 1/2 cup grated parmesan
- 2 teaspoons old bay seasoning
- 1/2 teaspoon garlic powder
- olive oil spray if needed

Directions:

1. Salt and pepper the cod strips.
2. Create a breading station for the fish. In one bowl add the flour. In the second bowl whisk together the eggs and salt. In the last bowl, add the Panko, parmesan cheese, old bay seasoning, and garlic powder.
3. First dip the cod in the flour, then the egg, and lastly the Panko mix.
4. Spray the bottom of your basket with olive oil. Place the fish in the basket of your air fryer. Cook at 400 degrees for 10 minutes. Continue to cook for 3-5 minutes or until the internal temperature reaches 145 degrees.

Nutritional Value (Amount per Serving):

Calories: 712; Fat: 51.69; Carb: 19.05; Protein: 40.05

Honey Glazed Salmon | Air Fryer Honey Glazed Salmon Recipe

Prep Time: 10 Mins   Cook Time: 10 Mins   Serves: 4

Ingredients:

- 16 oz Salmon Filets
- 3 tbsp Honey
- 2 tbsp Soy Sauce
- 2 tbsp Olive Oil
- 2 tbsp Minced Garlic
- 1 tsp Ginger
- 1/2 tsp Black Pepper
- 1/2 tsp Red Pepper Flakes
- lemon or lime, For Garnish
- Green Onion, For Garnish

Directions:

1. Prepare the Glaze. In a small bowl, whisk together the honey, soy sauce, olive oil, minced garlic, grated ginger, ground black pepper, and red pepper flakes (if using). This delectable glaze will be the key to imparting rich flavor and a beautiful caramelization to the salmon.
2. Marinate the Salmon. Place the salmon fillets in a shallow dish or a resealable plastic bag. Pour half of the honey glaze over the salmon, reserving the other half for basting during cooking. Make sure the salmon is evenly coated with the glaze. Cover the dish or seal the bag and refrigerate for at least 30 minutes to allow the flavors to infuse into the salmon.
3. Heat your air fryer oven to 400°F for a few minutes to ensure it's nice and hot before cooking the salmon.
4. Air Fry the Salmon. Remove the salmon from the marinade and shake off any excess liquid. Place the salmon fillets in the air fryer oven, making sure they are not touching. Air fry the salmon for 8-10 minutes, depending on the thickness of the fillets. Baste the salmon with the reserved honey glaze halfway through the cooking time to enhance the flavor.
5. Serve and Garnish. Once the salmon is cooked to perfection, remove it from the air fryer oven and transfer it to a serving plate. Garnish with fresh lemon slices and chopped green onions for a burst of freshness and a pop of color.

Nutritional Value (Amount per Serving):

Calories: 537; Fat: 21.24; Carb: 18.58; Protein: 69.91

Crab Rangoon Recipe | Air Fryer Crab Rangoon

Prep Time: 15 Mins   Cook Time: 8 Mins   Serves: 24 crab Rangoon

Ingredients:

- 8 ounces lump crab meat
- 8 ounces cream cheese
- 2 green onions
- 1 tsp minced garlic
- 1 tsp soy sauce
- 1/2 tsp Worcestershire sauce
- 1/4 tsp Ground Ginger
- 1/4 tsp White Pepper
- 24 Wonton Wrappers
- Cooking Spray

Directions:

1. In a mixing bowl, combine the softened cream cheese, minced garlic, chopped green onions, soy sauce, Worcestershire sauce, ground ginger, and white pepper. Mix until all the ingredients are well incorporated. Gently fold in the flaked crabmeat, being careful not to break up the meat too much. The mixture should be evenly combined, with visible chunks of crabmeat throughout.
2. Place the filling in the center of the wrapper and fold it up tight using the steps provided below.
3. Heat your air fryer oven to 375°F for about 5 minutes. Lightly spray a baking sheet with non-stick cooking spray to prevent sticking. Arrange the crab rangoon in a single layer on the sheet, making sure they are not touching each other. Lightly spray the crab rangoon with non-stick cooking spray. Place the baking sheet in the air fryer and cook for 8-10 minutes or until the crab rangoon are golden brown and crispy. Flip them halfway through the cooking time for even browning.
4. Allow the crab rangoon to cool for a few minutes before serving, as the filling can be extremely hot. Serve the Crab Rangoon on a platter, alongside a dipping sauce of your choice.

Nutritional Value (Amount per Serving):

Calories: 155; Fat: 3.55; Carb: 23.34; Protein: 7.56

Air Fried Salt and Pepper Shrimp

Prep Time: 10 Mins   Cook Time: 10 Mins   Serves: 4

Ingredients:

- 2 teaspoons Whole Black Peppercorns, ground
- 2 teaspoons Sichuan peppercorns, ground
- 1 teaspoon Kosher Salt
- 1 teaspoon Sugar Or Other Sweetener Equivalent

- 1 pound Shrimp, 21-25 per pound
- 3 tablespoons Rice Flour
- 2 tablespoons Oil

Directions:

1. Heat a saucepan on medium heat and roast the black peppercorns and sichuan peppercorns together for 1-2 minutes until you can smell the aroma from the peppercorns. Allow them to cool.
2. Add salt and sugar, and using a mortar and pestle, crush the spices together to form a coarse powder.
3. Place shrimp in a large bowl. Add the spices, rice flour and oil, and mix well until the shrimp are well-coated.
4. Place the shrimp in the air fryer oven, trying to keep them in as flat a layer as possible.
5. Spray well with additional oil.
6. Set the air fryer oven to 325°F and cook for 8-10 minutes, tossing halfway through.

Nutritional Value (Amount per Serving):

Calories: 216; Fat: 9.31; Carb: 5.84; Protein: 25.66

Air Fryer Keto Salmon Bok Choy Recipe

Prep Time: 20 Mins   Cook Time: 12 Mins   Serves: 2

Ingredients:

- 2 Garlic Cloves, minced
- 1 tablespoon Minced Ginger
- 2 teaspoons finely grated orange zest
- 1/2 cup fresh orange juice
- 1/4 cup Soy Sauce
- 3 tablespoons Rice Vinegar
- 1 tablespoon Vegetable Oil
- 1/2 teaspoon Kosher Salt
- 2 5 ounces Salmon Fillets
- For the Vegetables
- 2 heads baby bok choy, halved lenghtwise
- 2 ounces Dried Shiitake Mushrooms, stemmed (stems discarded)
- 1 tablespoon Dark Sesame Oil
- Kosher Salt
- 1/2 teaspoon Sesame Seeds, toasted

Directions:

1. For the fish: In a small bowl whisk together garlic, ginger, orange zest

and juice, soy sauce, vinegar, vegetable oil, and salt. Remove half of the marinade and reserve. Place salmon in a gallon-size resealable bag. Pour remaining half of marinade over salmon. Seal and massage to coat. Allow to marinate at room temperature for 30 minutes.

2. Place salmon in air fryer oven. Set fryer to 400°F for 12 minutes.
3. Meanwhile, for the vegetables: Brush bok choy and mushroom caps all over with sesame oil and season lightly with salt. After 6 minutes of cook time, add vegetables around salmon in air fryer oven. Continue cooking for remaining 6 minutes.
4. Drizzle salmon with some of the reserved marinade and sprinkle vegetables with sesame seeds to serve.

Nutritional Value (Amount per Serving):

Calories: 837; Fat: 35.44; Carb: 90.24; Protein: 38.23

Fish en Papillote | Air Fryer Fish in Parchment paper

Prep Time: 10 Mins   Cook Time: 15 Mins   Serves: 2

Ingredients:

- 2 5-oz. Cod Fillets, thawed
- 1/2 cup julienned carrots
- 1/2 cup julienned fennel bulbs, or 1/4 cup julienned celery
- 1/2 cup thinly sliced red peppers
- 2 sprigs tarragon, or 1/2 teaspoon dried tarragon
- 2 pats melted butter
- 1 tablespoon Lemon Juice
- 1 tablespoon Kosher Salt, divided
- 1/2 teaspoon Ground Black Pepper
- 1 tablespoon Oil

Directions:

1. In a medium bowl combine melted butter, tarragon, 1/2 teaspoon salt, and lemon juice. Mix well until you get a creamy sauce. Add the julienned vegetable and mix well. Set aside.
2. Cut two squares of parchment large enough to hold the fish and vegetables.
3. Spray the fish fillets with oil and apply salt and pepper to both sides of the fillets.
4. Lay one filet down on each parchment square. Top each fillet with half the vegetables. Pour any remaining sauce over the vegetables.
5. Fold over the parchment paper and crimp the sides to hold fish, veggies and sauce securely inside the packet. Place the packets inside the air fryer oven.

6. Set your air fryer to 350F for 15 minutes. Remove each packet to a plate and open just before serving.

Nutritional Value (Amount per Serving):

Calories: 266; Fat: 15.68; Carb: 6.12; Protein: 25.08

Air Fryer Cajun Shrimp

Prep Time: 10 Mins   Cook Time: 10 Mins   Serves: 4

Ingredients:

- FOR THE SAUCE
- 1/2 cup Mayonnaise
- 1 Garlic Cloves, minced
- 2 teaspoons Lemon Juice
- 2 tablespoons creole mustard
- 1/2 teaspoon hot pepper sauce
- 1 tablespoon sweet pickle relish
- 1 Chopped Green Scallions, chopped
- 1/2 teaspoons Worcestershire Sauce
- 1/4 teaspoon Smoked Paprika
- 1/4 teaspoon Kosher Salt
- FOR THE SHRIMP
- 1/2 cup Half and Half
- 1 Eggs
- 1 tablespoon Cajun Seasoning, without salt, divided
- 1 1/2 cups finely ground cornmeal
- 1 pound Raw Shrimp, large, peeled and deveined, 21-25 count
- Kosher Salt, to taste
- Ground Black Pepper, to taste
- Vegetable

Directions:

FOR THE SAUCE
1. In a small bowl combine the mayonnaise, garlic, mustard, hot pepper sauce, relish, green onion, Worcestershire sauce, paprika, and salt. Stir until well combined. Cover and chill until serving time.

FOR THE SHRIMP
1. In a large bowl, whisk together the half and half, egg, and 1 teaspoon of the Cajun seasoning. Add the shrimp and toss gently to combine. Refrigerate for at least 15 minutes or up to 1 hour.
2. Meanwhile, in a shallow dish, whisk together the cornmeal, remaining 2 teaspoons Cajun seasoning, and salt and pepper to taste.

3. Spray a cooking pan with vegetable oil spray. Dredge the shrimp in the cornmeal mixture until well-coated. Shake off any excess and arrange in a single layer the air-fryer oven. Spray shrimp with vegetable oil spray.
4. Set the air fryer oven to 350°F for 10 minutes, carefully turning and spraying the shrimp with vegetable oil spray halfway through the cooking time.
5. Serve the shrimp with the sauce.

Nutritional Value (Amount per Serving):

Calories: 604; Fat: 22.97; Carb: 53.84; Protein: 42.66

Keto Shrimp Scampi

Prep Time: 5 Mins   Cook Time: 10 Mins   Serves: 2

Ingredients:

- 4 tablespoons Butter
- 1 tablespoon Lemon Juice
- 1 tablespoon Minced Garlic
- 2 teaspoons Pepper Flakes
- 1 tablespoon chopped chives, or 1 teaspoon dried chives
- 1 tablespoon chopped fresh basil, or 1 teaspoon dried basil
- 2 tablespoons Chicken Stock, (or white wine)
- 1 lb Raw Shrimp, (21-25 count)

Directions:

1. Turn your air fryer oven to 330°F. Place a 6 x 3 metal pan in it and allow it to start heating while you gather your ingredients.
2. Place the butter, garlic, and red pepper flakes into the hot 6-inch pan.
3. Allow it to cook for 2 minutes, stirring once, until the butter has melted. Do not skip this step. This is what infuses garlic into the butter, which is what makes it all taste so good.
4. Open the air fryer oven, add butter, lemon juice, minced garlic, red pepper flakes, chives, basil, chicken stock, and shrimp to the pan in the order listed, stirring gently.
5. Allow shrimp to cook for 5 minutes, stirring once. At this point, the butter should be well-melted and liquid, bathing the shrimp in spiced goodness.
6. Mix very well, remove the 6-inch pan using silicone mitts, and let it rest for 1 minute on the counter. You're doing this so that you let the shrimp cook in the residual heat, rather than letting it accidentally overcook and get rubbery.
7. Stir at the end of the minute. The shrimp should be well-cooked at this point.

8. Sprinkle additional fresh basil leaves and enjoy.

Nutritional Value (Amount per Serving):

Calories: 401; Fat: 18.83; Carb: 6.78; Protein: 48.87

Salmon Croquettes | Air Fryer Salmon Patties

Prep Time: 10 Mins   Cook Time: 15 Mins   Serves: 2

Ingredients:

- 2 5 ounces pouches Salmon Packets, wild-caught
- 1 large Eggs, beaten
- 4 tablespoons Panko
- 1 Chopped Green Scallions, finely chopped, white and light green parts
- 1 teaspoon Dried Dill
- 1/2 teaspoon Kosher Salt
- 1/2 teaspoon Ground Black Pepper
- Cooking Oil Spray
- Lemon, wedges

Directions:

1. In a large bowl, combine the salmon, egg, bread crumbs, scallion, dillweed, and salt and black pepper to taste. Gently mix until well-combined. Form into 4 patties.
2. Spray a baking sheet with cooking spray. Lightly mist both sides of the patties with cooking spray.
3. Arrange the patties in the air fryer oven. Set the air fryer to 400°F for 15 minutes. Halfway through the cooking time, turn the patties and spray both sides with more vegetable oil spray. When done, patties should be golden-brown and crisp.
4. Serve croquettes hot with lemon wedges.

Nutritional Value (Amount per Serving):

Calories: 386; Fat: 25.52; Carb: 5.52; Protein: 32.77

Air Fryer Shrimp Fajitas

Prep Time: 10 Mins   Cook Time: 22 Mins   Serves: 12

Ingredients:

- 1 Red Bell Pepper Diced
- 1 Green Bell Pepper Diced
- 1/2 Cup Sweet Onion Diced

- 2 Tbsp of Gluten-Free Fajita or Taco Seasoning
- 1 Pound Medium Shrimp Tail-Off (Cooked, Frozen Shrimp)
- Olive Oil Spray
- White Corn Tortillas or Flour Tortillas

Directions:

1. Spray a baking sheet with olive oil spray or line with foil.
2. If the shrimp is frozen with ice on it, run cold water over it to get the ice off.
3. Add the peppers, onion, and seasoning to the baking sheet.
4. Add a coat of olive oil spray.
5. Mix it all together.
6. Cook at 390 degrees for 12 minutes using the air fry function.
7. Open the lid, and add in the shrimp for the final 10 minutes, spray it again, and mix it together.
8. Cook an additional 10 minutes.
9. Serve on warm tortillas.
10. This recipe uses cooked, frozen shrimp, it can be made with uncooked shrimp too, but may need a few additional minutes of cook time.

Nutritional Value (Amount per Serving):

Calories: 166; Fat: 7.66; Carb: 22.97; Protein: 2.74

Cajun Shrimp Boil in the Air Fryer

Prep Time: 10 Mins   Cook Time: 12 Mins   Serves: 6

Ingredients:

- 12 Oz Medium Shrimp
- 14 Oz Smoked Sausage Rope Sliced
- 4 Cups Par-Boiled Small Potatoes Halved
- 4 Mini Corn on the Cobs Quartered
- 1/4 Cup White Onion Diced
- 1/8 Cup Old Bay Seasoning or to Taste
- Olive Oil Spray

Directions:

1. Begin by making sure the potatoes have been par-boiled. We used small potatoes, cut in half for this recipe.
2. Once the potatoes are done, combine the remaining ingredients into a large bowl, mixing well. (Shrimp can be frozen)
3. Place a sheet of foil into your air fryer oven.
4. Add in about 1/2 of the mixture on top of the foil to fill the baking pan.
5. Once the ingredients are added, spray with a nice coat of olive oil spray.

6. Cook at 390 degrees for 6 minutes.
7. Open up the air fryer oven, carefully mix the ingredients.
8. Cook for an additional 6 minutes.
9. Repeat these steps for the next batch if needed.
10. Serve.

Nutritional Value (Amount per Serving):

Calories: 628; Fat: 39.88; Carb: 55.39; Protein: 18.33

Air Fryer Catfish

Prep Time: 5 Mins   Cook Time: 20 Mins   Serves: 4

Ingredients:

- 4 Catfish Fillets or Catfish Nuggets
- 1/2 Cup Gluten Free Fish Fry
- Olive Oil Cooking Spray

Directions:

1. Coat each catfish fillet or nugget with an even coat of fish fry.
2. Place in the air fryer oven and spray the olive oil spray on one side of the catfish.
3. Cook at 390°F for 10 minutes.
4. Carefully flip the catfish, coat with spray, and cook for an additional 10 minutes.
5. Serve.

Nutritional Value (Amount per Serving):

Calories: 397; Fat: 31.79; Carb: 0.02; Protein: 26.04

Gluten Free Air Fryer Honey Garlic Shrimp Recipe

Prep Time: 10 Mins   Cook Time: 20 Mins   Serves: 6

Ingredients:

- 1/2 cup Honey
- 1/2 cup Tamari Gluten Free Soy Sauce
- 2 tablespoons Ketchup
- 1 clove Garlic, crushed
- 1 teaspoon Fresh Ginger
- 2 tablespoons Cornstarch
- 16 ounces Fresh Shrimp, medium, peeled and deveined
- 16 ounces Frozen Mixed Stir-fry Vegetable Blend
- Cooked Rice, optional

Directions:

1. In a medium sized saucepan, add in the honey, soy sauce, ketchup, garlic, and ginger.
2. Let this warm up to a low-boil, whisk in the cornstarch until the sauce has thickened.
3. Coat the shrimp with the sauce.
4. Line an air fryer oven baking sheet with foil, and then add in the shrimp and vegetables.
5. Cook at 355°F for 10 Minutes.
6. Serve over cooked rice.

Nutritional Value (Amount per Serving):

Calories: 222; Fat: 1.6; Carb: 34.02; Protein: 20.33

Air Fryer Shrimp and Vegetables

Prep Time: 5 Mins   Cook Time: 20 Mins   Serves: 4

Ingredients:

- Small Shrimp Raw Peeled & Deveined (Regular Size Bag about 50-80 Small Shrimp)
- 1 Bag of Frozen Mixed Vegetables
- 1 Tbsp Gluten Free Cajun Seasoning
- Olive Oil Spray
- Cooked Rice

Directions:

1. Add the shrimp and vegetables to your air fryer oven.
2. Top it with the Cajun seasoning and spray with an even coat of spray.
3. Cook on 355 degrees for 10 minutes.
4. Carefully open and mix up the shrimp and vegetables.
5. Continue cooking for an additional 10 minutes on 355 degrees.
6. Serve over cooked rice.

Nutritional Value (Amount per Serving):

Calories: 121; Fat: 7.49; Carb: 13.17; Protein: 0.42

Chapter 6: Vegetables and Sides

Air Fryer Zucchini Chips

Prep Time: 5 Mins   Cook Time: 8 Mins   Serves: 4

Ingredients:

- 3 medium sized zucchinis
- 1 Tablespoon olive oil
- 1/4 teaspoon paprika
- salt and pepper

Directions:

1. Start by slicing your zucchini into 1/8 inch thickness with a mandolin. Pat to dry with a paper towel.
2. In a medium sized bowl add the zucchini, olive oil, paprika, and salt and pepper.
3. Lay the zucchini in a single layer in the air fryer basket.
4. Cook at 350 degrees for 4-5 minutes. Flip the chips and fry for an additional 2-3 minutes. Check the chips frequently to make sure that they don't burn.

Nutritional Value (Amount per Serving):

Calories: 37; Fat: 3.46; Carb: 1.45; Protein: 0.41

Air Fryer Green Beans with Parmesan

Prep Time: 5 Mins   Cook Time: 10 Mins   Serves: 6

Ingredients:

- 1 pound green beans
- 2 tablespoons olive oil
- 2 tablespoons lemon juice
- 1/4 cup grated parmesan
- 1 teaspoon garlic powder
- 1/2 teaspoon salt
- 1/4 teaspoon pepper

Directions:

1. In a bowl, add the green beans, olive oil, lemon juice, parmesan, garlic powder, salt, and pepper.
2. Stir everything together until combined.
3. Add it to your air fryer basket and cook at 370 degrees for 5 minutes.
4. Shake the basket, then cook for another 5 minutes or until golden and tender.

Nutritional Value (Amount per Serving):

Calories: 72; Fat: 5.03; Carb: 5.5; Protein: 2.32

Air Fryer Stuffed Peppers

Prep Time: 15 Mins   Cook Time: 15 Mins   Serves: 4

Ingredients:

- 4 whole bell peppers
- 1 tablespoon olive oil
- 1 small onion diced
- 1 pound lean ground beef
- 1 15 ounce can of diced tomatoes
- 1 8 ounce can of tomato sauce
- 2 cups rice cooked
- 1 Tablespoon Italian Seasoning
- 1 teaspoon garlic powder
- salt and pepper
- 2 cups Colby Jack cheese shredded

Directions:

1. To prepare the peppers, slice the tops off and remove any veins or seeds inside. In a medium sized saucepan over medium high heat, add the olive oil and onion. Cook until almost tender. Add in the ground beef, and cook and crumble until no longer pink.
2. Add in the diced tomatoes, tomato sauce, rice, Italian seasoning, garlic powder, and salt and pepper.
3. Stuff the peppers with the mixture, and place in the basket of the air fryer.
4. Cook the peppers at 360 degrees until tender for 10 minutes. Top with cheese, and then cook for an additional 2-3 minutes.

Nutritional Value (Amount per Serving):

Calories: 791; Fat: 46.48; Carb: 53.96; Protein: 55.43

Air Fryer Frozen Broccoli

Prep Time:2 Mins   Cook Time: 10 Mins   Serves: 4

Ingredients:

- 16 ounces Frozen Broccoli Florets
- Salt & Pepper to taste
- Olive Oil, to drizzle (optional)

Directions:

1. Place frozen broccoli into the basket of the air fryer.
2. Close the basket and air fry the broccoli for 10 minutes at 400 degrees Fahrenheit.
3. Shake the basket halfway through to evenly cook the broccoli.
4. Continue to cook for an additional 1-2 minutes if you want your broccoli crispier.
5. Once the broccoli is cooked to your liking, drizzle with olive oil, and season with salt and pepper. Enjoy as a side to any entree!

Nutritional Value (Amount per Serving):

Calories: 92; Fat: 7.68; Carb: 4.3; Protein: 3.82

Air Fryer Vegetables

Prep Time: 5 Mins   Cook Time: 10 Mins   Serves: 4

Ingredients:

- 1 cup broccoli florets
- 1 red bell pepper chopped
- 6 ounces mushrooms sliced
- 1 small zucchini sliced
- 1 small yellow squash sliced
- 2 Tablespoons olive oil
- 1 Tablespoon Italian seasoning
- 1 Tablespoon grated parmesan cheese

Directions:

1. In a medium-sized bowl, add the broccoli florets, bell pepper, mushrooms, zucchini, and yellow squash.
2. Add the olive oil, Italian seasoning, and parmesan and toss.
3. Place vegetables in the basket of the air fryer. Cook at 390 degrees for 5 minutes. Open the air fryer and toss the vegetables. Continue to cook for 5 minutes or until tender.

Nutritional Value (Amount per Serving):

Calories: 89; Fat: 7.33; Carb: 4.33; Protein: 2.4

Air Fryer Potato Wedges Recipe

Prep Time: 10 Mins   Cook Time: 20 Mins   Serves: 4

Ingredients:

- 3 Russet or Yukon Gold potatoes
- 1 ½ tablespoons olive oil
- ½ teaspoon kosher salt
- ½ teaspoon garlic powder
- ½ teaspoon ground black pepper
- ½ teaspoon chili powder
- ½ teaspoon dried parsley flakes
- Grated Parmesan cheese, ketchup, aioli, or favorite dipping sauce for serving

Directions:

1. Heat air fryer oven to 400°F for 5 minutes.
2. Wash and scrub the potatoes and dry thoroughly. On a cutting board, cut each potato in half lengthwise. Cut each half in half again, and then in half one more time for a total of 8 wedges.
3. Place the potato wedges into a large bowl. Drizzle with olive oil and toss to coat evenly.

4. Add the spices and mix until evenly combined.
5. Place the seasoned potato wedges into the air fryer oven.
6. Reduce the heat to 380°F and cook for 20 minutes, flipping the wedges halfway through cooking.
7. Serve immediately with grated Parmesan cheese and your favorite dipping sauces.

Nutritional Value (Amount per Serving):

Calories: 273; Fat: 5.71; Carb: 51.19; Protein: 6.51

Air-Fried Ratatouille, Italian-Style

Prep Time:25 Mins   Cook Time:25 Mins   Serves 4

Ingredients:

- ½ small eggplant, cut into cubes
- 1 zucchini, cut into cubes
- 1 medium tomato, cut into cubes
- ½ large yellow bell pepper, cut into cubes
- ½ large red bell pepper, cut into cubes
- ½ onion, cut into cubes
- 1 fresh cayenne pepper, diced
- 5 sprigs fresh basil, stemmed and chopped
- 2 sprigs fresh oregano, stemmed and chopped
- 1 clove garlic, crushed
- salt and ground black pepper to taste
- 1 tablespoon olive oil
- 1 tablespoon white wine
- 1 teaspoon vinegar

Directions:

1. Heat an air fryer oven to 400 degrees F.
2. Place eggplant, zucchini, tomato, bell peppers, and onion in a bowl. Add cayenne pepper, basil, oregano, garlic, salt, and pepper. Mix well to distribute everything evenly. Drizzle in oil, wine, and vinegar, mixing to coat all the vegetables.
3. Pour vegetable mixture into a baking dish and insert it into the air fryer. Cook for 8 minutes. Stir; cook for another 8 minutes. Stir again and continue cooking until tender, stirring every 5 minutes, 10 to 15 more minutes. Turn off the air fryer, leaving the dish inside. Let rest for 5 minutes before serving.

Nutritional Value (Amount per Serving):

Calories: 75; Fat: 3.91; Carb: 10.19; Protein: 1.96

Rosemary Potato Wedges for the Air Fryer

Prep Time: 10 Mins   Cook Time: 20 Mins   Serves: 4

Ingredients:

- 2 russet potatoes, sliced into 12 wedges each with skin on
- 1 tablespoon extra-virgin olive oil
- 2 teaspoons seasoned salt
- 1 tablespoon finely chopped fresh rosemary

Directions:

1. Heat an air fryer oven to 380 degrees F.
2. Place potatoes in a large bowl and toss with olive oil. Sprinkle with seasoned salt and rosemary and toss to combine.
3. Place potatoes in an even layer in fryer once air fryer oven is hot; you may need to cook them in batches.
4. Air fry potatoes for 10 minutes, then flip wedges with tongs. Continue air frying until potato wedges reach the desired doneness, about 10 more minutes.

Nutritional Value (Amount per Serving):

Calories: 160; Fat: 1.67; Carb: 33.43; Protein: 3.98

Potato Hay

Prep Time: 10 Mins   Cook Time: 30 Mins   Serves: 4

Ingredients:

- 2 russet potatoes
- 1 tablespoon canola oil
- kosher salt and ground black pepper to taste

Directions:

1. Cut potatoes into spirals using the medium grating attachment on a spiralizer, cutting the spirals with kitchen shears after 4 or 5 rotations.
2. Soak potato spirals in a bowl of water for 20 minutes. Drain and rinse well. Pat potatoes dry with paper towels, removing as much moisture as possible.
3. Place potato spirals in a large resealable plastic bag. Add oil, salt, and pepper; toss to coat.
4. Heat an air fryer to 360 degrees F.
5. Place 1/2 of the potato spirals in the frier. Cook until golden, about 5 minutes.
6. Increase temperature to 390 degrees F. Pull out the frying sheet and toss potato spirals using tongs. Return to the air fryer and continue cooking,

tossing occasionally, until golden brown, 10 to 12 minutes.

7. Reduce temperature to 360 degrees F and repeat with remaining potato spirals.

Nutritional Value (Amount per Serving):

Calories: 181; Fat: 3.67; Carb: 34.4; Protein: 4.17

Air Fryer Roasted Cauliflower

Prep Time: 10 Mins   Cook Time: 15 Mins   Serves: 2

Ingredients:

- 3 cloves garlic
- 1 tablespoon peanut oil
- ½ teaspoon salt
- ½ teaspoon smoked paprika
- 4 cups cauliflower florets

Directions:

1. Gather all ingredients.
2. Heat an air fryer oven to 400 degrees F according to manufacturer's instructions.
3. Cut garlic in half and smash with the blade of a knife. Place in a bowl with oil, salt, and paprika. Add cauliflower and toss to coat.
4. Place coated cauliflower on a baking sheet in the air fryer oven, and cook to desired crispness, about 15 minutes, shaking the baking tray every 5 minutes.

Nutritional Value (Amount per Serving):

Calories: 122; Fat: 7.45; Carb: 12.45; Protein: 4.48

Air Fryer Baked Potatoes

Prep Time: 5 Mins   Cook Time: 1 Hr   Serves: 2

Ingredients:

- 2 large russet potatoes, scrubbed
- 1 tablespoon peanut oil
- ½ teaspoon coarse sea salt

Directions:

1. Heat an air fryer oven to 400 degrees F.
2. Brush potatoes with peanut oil, sprinkle with salt, and place them in the air fryer.
3. Cook potatoes until very tender when pierced with a fork, about 1 hour.

Nutritional Value (Amount per Serving):

Calories: 351; Fat: 7.05; Carb: 66.68; Protein: 7.9

Air Fryer Roasted Broccoli and Cauliflower

Prep Time:10 Mins   Cook Time:15 Mins   Serves: 6

Ingredients:

- 3 cups broccoli florets
- 3 cups cauliflower florets
- 2 tablespoons olive oil
- ½ teaspoon garlic powder
- ¼ teaspoon sea salt
- ¼ teaspoon paprika
- ⅛ teaspoon ground black pepper

Directions:

1. Heat an air fryer oven to 400 degrees F.
2. Place broccoli florets in a large, microwave-safe bowl. Cook in the microwave at full power for 3 minutes; drain any accumulated liquid.
3. Add cauliflower, olive oil, garlic powder, sea salt, paprika, and black pepper to the bowl with broccoli; mix well to combine. Pour mixture onto a baking tray in the air fryer oven.
4. Cook in the preheated air fryer for 12 minutes, tossing vegetables halfway through cooking time for even browning.

Nutritional Value (Amount per Serving):

Calories: 59; Fat: 4.76; Carb: 3.57; Protein: 1.74

Chapter 7: Appetizers and Snacks

Hot Spinach Artichoke Dip

Prep Time: 10 Mins   Cook Time: 15 Mins   Serves: 12

Ingredients:

- 8 ounce cream cheese softened
- 1/2 cup sour cream
- 1/4 cup mayonnaise
- 3 garlic cloves minced
- 1/2 cup mozzarella cheese shredded
- 1 cup Parmesan Cheese grated
- 1 14 ounce can Artichokes chopped
- 6 ounce frozen spinach thawed

Directions:

1. Heat oven to 400 degrees. In a medium sized bowl, add the cream cheese, sour cream, and mayonnaise and mix until incorporated. Add the garlic, mozzarella cheese, parmesan, artichokes and spinach.
2. Spread the mixture evenly into a 1 quart baking dish. Bake for 15-20 minutes or until it is heated through and bubbly. Serve warm with sliced baguette or crackers.

Nutritional Value (Amount per Serving):

Calories: 147; Fat: 10.46; Carb: 7.14; Protein: 7.48

Air Fryer Bacon-Wrapped Stuffed Jalapenos

Prep Time: 10 Mins   Cook Time: 14 Mins   Serves: 6

Ingredients:

- 12 Jalapenos
- 8 ounces of cream cheese, room temperature or slightly soft
- 1/2 cup shredded cheddar cheese
- 1/4 teaspoon garlic powder
- 1/8 teaspoon onion powder
- 12 slices of bacon, thinly cut
- salt and pepper to taste

Directions:

1. Cut the jalapenos in half, remove the stems, and remove the seeds and membranes. The more membrane you leave, the spicier the jalapenos will be.
2. Add cream cheese, shredded cheddar cheese, garlic powder, onion powder, salt, and pepper in a bowl. Mix to combine.
3. Using a small spoon, scoop the cream mixture into each jalapeno, filling it just to the top.
4. Heat air fryer to 350 degrees for about 3 minutes.
5. Cut each slice of bacon in half.

6. Wrap each jalapeno half in one piece of bacon.
7. Place the bacon-wrapped stuffed jalapenos in the air fryer in an even layer, making sure they do not touch.
8. Air fry at 350 degrees for 14-16 minutes, until bacon is thoroughly cooked.
9. Enjoy immediately, or refrigerate for up to 3 days, reheating before eating.

Nutritional Value (Amount per Serving):

Calories: 336; Fat: 31.48; Carb: 4.09; Protein: 9.79

Air Fryer Ravioli

Prep Time: 5 Mins   Cook Time: 6 Mins   Serves: 2

Ingredients:

- 12 frozen ravioli
- 1/2 cup buttermilk
- 1/2 cup Italian breadcrumbs
- ALSO
- Marinara sauce for dipping
- Oil for spritzing

Directions:

1. Heat air fryer to 400 degrees.
2. Place two bowls side by side. Put the buttermilk in one and breadcrumbs in the other.
3. Dip each piece of ravioli into the buttermilk then breadcrumbs, making sure to coat as best as possible.
4. Place each breaded ravioli into the air fryer in one single layer, and cook for 6-7 minutes, spritzing the tops with oil halfway through.
5. Remove from the air fryer and enjoy immediately with marinara, or freeze for up to 3 months.

Nutritional Value (Amount per Serving):

Calories: 458; Fat: 22.39; Carb: 51.89; Protein: 14.76

Mac And Cheese Bites In The Air Fryer

Prep Time: 10 Mins   Cook Time: 10 Mins   Freezing Time: 30 Mins
Serves: 15

Ingredients:

- 2 cups of cold leftover mac and cheese (I used this recipe with elbow noodles)
- 1 cup of italian bread crumbs
- 1/2 teaspoons salt
- 1/2 teaspoons garlic powder

- ½ teaspoons dried parsley
- 1/4 teaspoons paprika
- 2 eggs, beaten
- 1/2 cup of marinara for dipping

Directions:

1. Using cold leftover mac and cheese and a cookie scoop, scoop out the mac and cheese and then roll using the palm of your hand. Place them on a piece of parchment paper and once they are all rolled, place them in the freezer 30 minutes to an hour.
2. In a small bowl, mix the bread crumbs and seasonings.
3. In another small bowl, beat the eggs and set them aside.
4. When your mac and cheese balls are chilled, roll them into the egg mixture and then into the bread crumbs.
5. Heat your air fryer to 350 degrees. Spray the tops of the bites to make them extra crispy. Cook for 5 minutes, and then flip and cook for an additional 4-5 minutes till they are golden.

Nutritional Value (Amount per Serving):

Calories: 104; Fat: 7.89; Carb: 3.21; Protein: 5.07

Air Fryer Tortilla Chips

Prep Time: 5 Mins   Cook Time: 5 Mins   Serves: 2

Ingredients:

- 4 6-inch corn tortillas
- Avocado or olive oil spray
- ¼-½ teaspoon kosher salt

Directions:

1. Heat the air fryer to 350 degrees F for 5 minutes.
2. Lightly spray both sides of each tortilla with oil and sprinkle with salt. Use a pizza cutter or sharp knife to cut the tortillas into triangles (you should get 6-8 chips per tortilla).
3. Place the triangles in a single layer in the air fryer basket, and air fry for 3 minutes. Open the basket and flip the chips, the cook for an additional 1-2 minutes until they're crispy and golden brown.
4. Repeat with remaining tortillas until all are cooked.

Nutritional Value (Amount per Serving):

Calories: 1781; Fat: 35.7; Carb: 336.84; Protein: 42.73

Easy Air Fryer Wontons

Prep Time: 18 Mins   Cook Time: 12 Mins   Serves: 15

Ingredients:

- 8 ounces cream cheese, room temperature
- 1 green onion, thinly sliced
- 1 tablespoon powdered sugar
- ½ teaspoon toasted sesame oil
- ½ teaspoon garlic powder
- ¼ teaspoon kosher salt
- 15 wonton wrappers
- Sweet chili sauce, for serving

Directions:

1. In a mixing bowl, mix together the cream cheese, green onion, sugar, garlic powder, salt, and sesame oil.
2. Spoon 1 tablespoon of the filling in the middle of a wonton wrapper. Use your finger to dab a bit of water on the outer edges of the wrapper and fold two opposite corners together.
3. Fold the other two ends to create a small parcel, pinching the edges together to seal the wonton tightly.
4. Repeat with the remaining filling and wrappers.
5. Working in batches, place wontons in a single layer in the air fryer oven, leaving a little space between them. Spray them with a generous amount of cooking oil spray.
6. Air fry for 8-12 minutes until golden brown and crisp to your liking, flipping the wontons over halfway through the cooking time and spritzing the bottoms lightly with more oil.

Nutritional Value (Amount per Serving):

Calories: 144; Fat: 4.99; Carb: 20.28; Protein: 4.32

Air Fryer Lemon Pepper Wings

Prep Time: 5 Mins   Cook Time: 25 Mins   Serves: 4

Ingredients:

- 1 1/2 pounds chicken wings, drumettes and flats separated and tips discarded
- 2 teaspoons McCormick lemon pepper seasoning
- 1/4 teaspoon cayenne pepper
- FOR THE LEMON PEPPER SAUCE
- 3 tablespoons butter
- 1 teaspoon McCormicks lemon pepper seasoning
- 1 teaspoon honey

Directions:

1. Heat your air fryer oven to 380 degrees.
2. Coat the chicken wings with lemon pepper seasoning and cayenne pepper.
3. Place the lemon pepper wings in the air fryer oven, filling it no more than halfway full. Cook for 20-22 minutes, shaking the pan/sheet halfway through cooking.
4. Increase the temperature to 400 degrees and cook for an additional 3-5 minutes to get a nice crispy skin on the chicken wings.
5. While the chicken wings are cooking, mix the melted butter, additional lemon pepper seasoning, and honey in a bowl.
6. Remove chicken wings from the air fryer and drizzle the lemon honey sauce on top. Enjoy!

Nutritional Value (Amount per Serving):

Calories: 304; Fat: 14.73; Carb: 1.64; Protein: 39.05

Air Fryer Cheese Curds

Prep Time: 15 Mins   Cook Time: 30 Mins   Serves: 4-5

Ingredients:

- 16 ounces cheese curds
- 2 cups bread crumbs
- 2 teaspoons Italian seasoning
- ½ teaspoon salt
- ¼ teaspoon pepper
- 3 large eggs
- 1 tablespoon water
- ¼ cup all purpose flour

Directions:

1. In a wide, shallow bowl, whisk together the bread crumbs, Italian seasoning, salt, and pepper. In a second bowl, combine the eggs and water, whisking to combine.
2. Place the cheese curds in a large bowl and add the flour. Toss well to coat. Dredge the curds through the egg, then roll them in the bread crumb mixture, ensuring they are fully and evenly coated. Repeat the process a second time, double coating them in egg and crumbs. Place on a large plate.
3. Heat the air fryer to 400 degrees, then place half of the breaded cheese curds in an even layer on a baking sheet. Spray the tops with cooking spray and air fry at 400 degrees F for 5-6 minutes until heated through.
4. Repeat with remaining cheese curds, then serve with marinara sauce.

Nutritional Value (Amount per Serving):

Calories: 233; Fat: 8.93; Carb: 20; Protein: 17.11

Air Fryer Garlic Knots

Prep Time: 10 Mins   Cook Time: 5 Mins   Serves: 12

Ingredients:

- 1 Premade Pizza Dough
- 1 tablespoon Parmesan Cheese
- 1 tablespoon Olive Oil
- ½ teaspoon Garlic Powder
- ½ teaspoon Onion Powder
- ½ teaspoon Salt
- ¼ teaspoon Pepper
- ¼ teaspoon Red Pepper Flakes
- 1 tablespoon Chopped Fresh Parsley

Directions:

1. Roll out the premade pizza dough and slice them into 12 strips about 1 ½" to 2" wide.
2. Fold the dough in half so the rectangles measure 1"x12".
3. Fold them into a knot shape and wrap the ends under and over, making them into a circle knot shape.
4. Heat your air fryer to 360 degrees F
5. Add 6 dough knots into your air fryer oven on a baking sheet, making sure that there is space between each knot.
6. Cook them at 360 degrees F for 5 minutes.
7. While the knots are cooking, add the salt, pepper, garlic powder, onion powder, and red pepper flakes to a small bowl. Then add in the fresh chopped parsley and parmesan cheese.
8. Using a small whisk or fork, stir to combine the ingredients.
9. Remove the knots from the air fryer oven and bake the other 6 knots as you did before.
10. Once the knots are finished cooking, brush some olive oil over the top and sprinkle some of the garlic-parmesan mixture on the top as well.
11. Serve immediately with some pizza sauce, marinara sauce, or your favorite dipping sauce.

Nutritional Value (Amount per Serving):

Calories: 46; Fat: 2.25; Carb: 5.5; Protein: 1.07

Chapter 8: Desserts

Air Fryer Churros

Prep Time: 10 Mins   Cook Time: 10 Mins   Serves: 8

Ingredients:

- 1 cup water
- ⅓ cup unsalted butter, cut into cubes
- 2 Tbsp granulated sugar
- ¼ tsp salt
- 1 cup all-purpose flour
- 2 large eggs
- 1 tsp vanilla extract
- oil spray
- CINNAMON-SUGAR COATING:
- ½ cup granulated sugar
- ¾ tsp ground cinnamon

Directions:

1. Put a silicone baking mat on a baking sheet and spray with oil spray.
2. In a medium saucepan add water, butter, sugar, and salt. Bring to a boil over medium-high heat.
3. Reduce heat to medium-low and add flour to the saucepan. Stirring constantly with a rubber spatula cook until the dough comes together and is smooth.
4. Remove from heat and transfer the dough to a mixing bowl. Let cool for 4 minutes.
5. Add eggs and vanilla extract to the mixing bowl, and mix using an electric hand mixer or stand mixer until dough comes together. The mixture will look like gluey mashed potatoes. Use your hands to press lumps together into a ball, and transfer to a large piping bag fitted with a large star-shaped tip.
6. Pipe churros onto the greased baking mat, into 4-inch lengths, and cut end with scissors.
7. Refrigerate piped churros on the baking sheet for 1 hour.
8. Carefully transfer churros to the Air Fryer basket, leaving about ½-inch space between churros. Spray churros with oil spray. Depending on the size of your Air Fryer, you have to fry them in batches.
9. Air fry at 375 degrees F for 10-12 minutes until golden brown.
10. In a shallow bowl combine granulated sugar and cinnamon.
11. Immediately transfer baked churros to the bowl with the sugar mixture, and toss to coat. Working in batches. Serve warm with Nutella or chocolate dipping sauce.

Nutritional Value (Amount per Serving):

Calories: 182; Fat: 9.92; Carb: 20.57; Protein: 2.6

Air Fryer Apple Pies

Prep Time: 30 Mins   Cook Time: 15 Mins   Serves: 4

Ingredients:

- 2 medium Granny Smith apples, diced
- 6 tablespoons brown sugar
- 4 tablespoons butter
- 1 teaspoon ground cinnamon
- 1 teaspoon cornstarch
- 2 teaspoons cold water
- ½ (14 ounce) package pastry for a 9-inch double crust pie
- cooking spray
- ½ tablespoon grapeseed oil
- ¼ cup confectioners› sugar
- 1 teaspoon milk, or more as needed

Directions:

1. Combine apples, brown sugar, butter, and cinnamon in a nonstick skillet. Cook over medium heat until apples have softened, about 5 minutes.
2. Dissolve cornstarch in cold water. Stir into apple mixture and cook until sauce thickens, about 1 minute. Remove apple pie filling from heat and set aside to cool while you prepare the crust.
3. Unroll pie crust on a lightly floured surface and roll out slightly to smooth the surface of the dough. Cut dough into rectangles, small enough so that two can fit in your air fryer at one time. Repeat with remaining crust until you have 8 equal rectangles, re-rolling some of the scraps of dough if needed.
4. Wet the outer edges of 4 rectangles with water and place some apple filling in the center, about 1/2-inch from the edges. Roll out the remaining 4 rectangles so that they are slightly larger than the filled ones. Place these rectangles on top of the filling; crimp the edges with a fork to seal. Cut 4 small slits in the tops of the pies.
5. Heat an air fryer to 385 degrees F according to manufacturer's instructions.
6. Spray the basket of an air fryer with cooking spray. Brush the tops of 2 pies with oil, and transfer pies to the air fryer basket using a spatula.
7. Insert basket and bake in the heated air fryer until golden brown, about 8 minutes. Remove pies from the basket and repeat with the remaining 2 pies.
8. Mix together confectioners' sugar and milk in a small bowl. Brush glaze on warm pies and allow to dry. Serve pies warm or at room temperature.

Nutritional Value (Amount per Serving):

Calories: 353; Fat: 19.51; Carb: 43.87; Protein: 1.97

Easy Air Fryer Lemon Pound Cake Dessert

Prep Time: 20 Mins   Cook Time: 30-35 Mins   Serves: 4

Ingredients:

- 1 ½ cups All-Purpose Flour
- 1 teaspoon Baking Powder
- ½ teaspoon Salt
- ½ cup Softened Unsalted Butter (at room temperature)
- 1 cup Sweetener
- 4 Eggs
- 1 tablespoon Lemon Zest
- 2 tablespoons Fresh-Squeezed Lemon Juice
- 1 teaspoon Vanilla Extract
- ⅔ cup Sour Cream (or plain Greek yogurt)
- 1 tablespoon Confectioner's Sweetener (Optional for dusting)

Directions:

1. You will need the right equipment. I used a 6 cup bundt pan from Amazon. Grease the pan really well, using a Cooking Spray for Baking.
2. Add flour, salt, and baking powder to a medium bowl.
3. Cream butter and sweetener together in a mixing bowl.
4. Add in eggs and mix.
5. Add the dry ingredients to the wet along with vanilla, lemon juice, Greek yogurt, and lemon zest. Mix.
6. Pour the batter into the cake pan.
7. Air Fry at 320 degrees.

Nutritional Value (Amount per Serving):

Calories: 687; Fat: 29.89; Carb: 86.64; Protein: 16.17

Air Fryer Cheesecake

Prep Time: 15 Mins   Cook Time: 1 Hr   Serves: 6

Ingredients:

- Crust
- ¾ cup graham cracker crumbs
- 2 tablespoons granulated sugar
- 2 tablespoons butter melted
- A dash of salt
- Cheesecake Filling
- 16 ounces cream cheese softened
- ½ cup sour cream
- ¾ cup granulated sugar
- 2 large eggs room temperature
- 1 teaspoon lemon zest

- 1 teaspoon vanilla extract

Directions:

Crust

1. Grease a 6-7 inch springform pan with cooking spray. Place a parchment round in the bottom.
2. Combine the graham cracker crumbs with the melted butter and salt, until it resembles wet sand. Press into the bottom of the pan, use your fingers or a flat-bottomed glass or measuring cup to press it in. If you're using a 6-inch pan, you may omit a tablespoon or two of the crust if desired.
3. Bake in the airfryer at 275 degrees fahrenheit for 10 minutes. Let cool completely.

Cheesecake Filling

1. Use a stand mixer or hand mixer to beat the softened cream cheese and sour cream until smooth. Add the sugar and beat again until combined, scraping down the sides and bottom of the bowl as needed.
2. Add the eggs one at a time, mixing each one just until incorporated. Add the lemon zest and vanilla, and beat until combined and smooth.
3. Pour the batter over the cooled crust and bake at 285 degrees fahrenheit for 30 minutes. After 30 minutes, bake at 250 degrees fahrenheit for 15-20 more minutes, until the cheesecake is set but still has a little wobble to it.
4. Crack open the airfryer and leave the cheesecake inside for 30-60 minutes, until the airfryer has cooled.
5. Chill the cheesecake in the fridge for 4 hours or overnight before removing from the pan and serving.

Nutritional Value (Amount per Serving):

Calories: 504; Fat: 37.31; Carb: 34.39; Protein: 8.89

Air Fryer French Toast

Prep Time: 3 Mins   Cook Time: 3 Mins   Serves: 4

Ingredients:

- 4 eggs
- 2/3 cup milk
- 1 1/2 teaspoon cinnamon
- 1 Tablespoon vanilla
- 4 slices thick bread Texas toast or French bread
- Optional Toppings
- fresh berries
- powdered sugar
- syrup

Directions:

1. In a medium size bowl, add eggs and milk and whisk together until smooth. Add in the cinnamon and vanilla and whisk.
2. Dip your french toast into the mixture. Then, add it to a baking sheet/pan. Cook at 350 degrees for 3-5 minutes, then flip. Cook for an additional 3-5 minutes or until golden.
3. Top with your favorite toppings, fresh berries, powdered sugar, and syrup and enjoy!

Nutritional Value (Amount per Serving):

Calories: 341; Fat: 16.83; Carb: 32.3; Protein: 13.03

Air Fryer Turtle Cheesecake

Prep Time: 20 Mins   Cook Time: 35 Mins   Serves: 8

Ingredients:

- 1 cup graham cracker crumbs
- 1 tablespoon sugar
- 6 tablespoons butter, melted
- 12 ounces cream cheese, softened
- 1/3 cup sour cream
- 1/3 cup sugar
- 1 teaspoon lemon juice
- 1 teaspoon vanilla extract
- 1 pinch salt
- 2 large eggs
- 2 tablespoons chocolate ice cream topping, or to taste
- 2 tablespoons caramel ice cream topping, or to taste
- 2 tablespoons chopped toasted pecans, or to taste

Directions:

1. Line the bottom of a 7- to 7 1/2-inch springform pan or cake pan with parchment paper.
2. Stir together graham crackers and 1 tablespoon sugar in a bowl. Stir in melted butter.
3. Press crumb mixture into the bottom and 1 inch up the sides of the prepared pan.
4. For the filling, combine cream cheese, sour cream, 1/3 cup sugar, lemon juice, vanilla, and salt in a bowl. Beat with an electric mixer at medium-high speed until smooth. Add eggs, 1 at a time, beating at low speed until just combined. Pour filling over the crust. Arrange pan in the air fryer oven.

5. Set air fryer to 300 degrees F.
6. Cook for 15 minutes. Reduce temperature to 240 degrees F and cook 20 more minutes. The center of the cheesecake will appear wet and may jiggle slightly. Transfer cheesecake to a wire rack. Let stand about 15 minutes. Using a small sharp knife or thin spatula, loosen cheesecake from sides of pan; let stand until completely cooled, about 30 more minutes. Remove cheesecake from pan. Chill, covered, at least 4 hours or up to overnight.
7. To serve, drizzle with chocolate and caramel, ice cream toppings, and sprinkle with pecans.

Nutritional Value (Amount per Serving):

Calories: 432; Fat: 31.24; Carb: 32; Protein: 7.31

Air Fryer Raspberry Brownie Bites

Prep Time: 25 Mins   Cook Time: 10 Mins   Serves: 20

Ingredients:

- 2/3 cup fresh or frozen raspberries
- 2 tablespoons cashew butter
- 2 tablespoons water
- 4 ounces dark chocolate, chopped
- 4 tablespoons unsalted butter
- 1/4 cup canola oil
- 1 large egg
- 1 large egg yolk
- 1/2 cup sugar
- 1 teaspoon vanilla extract
- 1/4 teaspoon salt
- 1/3 cup all purpose flour
- 1/3 cup whole-wheat pastry flour
- 2 tablespoons unsweetened cocoa powder

Directions:

1. Lightly coat 20 (13/4-inch) foil muffin cups with cooking spray.
2. Cook raspberries in a small saucepan over medium-low heat, stirring and crushing them with a fork, until broken down, 2 to 4 minutes. Transfer to a mini food processor. Add cashew butter and the water; purée until smooth.
3. Stir together dark chocolate, butter, and oil in a stainless-steel bowl. Set bowl over a saucepan of gently simmering water and melt ingredients, stirring occasionally. Remove from heat and stir until combined. Let cool about 20 minutes.
4. Combine egg, egg yolk, sugar, vanilla, and salt in another bowl. Beat with

an electric mixer at medium-high until thickened, 3 to 5 minutes.

5. In a small bowl, whisk together flours and cocoa powder. Fold flour mixture, half at a time, into egg mixture until incorporated. With mixer running at medium-low, mix in melted chocolate mixture until well combined.

6. Spoon 2 teaspoons brownie batter into each prepared muffin cup. Layer 1 teaspoon raspberry mixture followed by 1/2 teaspoon brownie batter over top of each. Working in batches if needed, arrange muffin cups in an even layer on a baking tray in the air fryer oven.

7. Heat air fryer to 350 degrees F.

8. Cook brownies in the air fryer oven until set, about 5 minutes. Remove and cool on a wire rack.

9. Brownies will keep chilled and covered for up to 3 days.

Nutritional Value (Amount per Serving):

Calories: 122; Fat: 8.14; Carb: 11.18; Protein: 1.63

Air Fryer Pizookie

Prep Time: 5 Mins   Cook Time: 10 Mins   Serves: 6

Ingredients:

- 5 pieces pre-cut refrigerated chocolate chip cookie dough
- 1 scoop vanilla gelato (optional)
- 2 tablespoons whipped cream, or as needed (optional)
- 1 ounce chocolate, melted, to drizzle (optional)

Directions:

1. Heat the air fryer oven to 360 degrees F.

2. Get a large piece of aluminum foil and fold it into an 8x8-inch square. You can make a little dish out of the foil by folding the edges upward.

3. Place 1 piece of cookie dough in the middle of your foil. Arrange remaining cookie dough pieces around it in a pattern similar to the 5-side of a die.

4. Bake cookies in the air fryer oven for 6 minutes. Open the air fryer oven and gently push down the top of the cookie; continue to bake until deep golden brown, 2 to 4 more minutes.

5. Add gelato, whipped cream, and a drizzle of melted chocolate, and enjoy!

Nutritional Value (Amount per Serving):

Calories: 322; Fat: 8.96; Carb: 56; Protein: 3.64

Air Fryer Waffle Egg in a Hole

Prep Time: 2 Mins   Cook Time: 8 Mins   Serves: 1

Ingredients:

- 1 frozen waffle
- 1 large egg
- salt and pepper to taste
- 2 tablespoons shredded cheese
- maple syrup to taste

Directions:

1. Heat the air fryer oven to 350 degrees F.
2. Cut a hole in the center of the frozen waffle using the rim of a cup or glass (about 2 to 3 inches in diameter). Move waffle to a square of parchment paper, then carefully place the parchment paper into the preheated air fryer oven, along with the small center waffle.
3. Crack egg directly into the center of waffle hole; season with salt and pepper to taste. Close the door and cook until the white of the egg has started to set, about 5 to 6 minutes.
4. Remove small center waffle from the air fryer. Sprinkle shredded cheese onto egg waffle, and cook until the cheese is melted and egg white is completely set, about 1 to 2 minutes.
5. Transfer egg waffle onto a plate; drizzle with maple syrup and serve immediately.

Nutritional Value (Amount per Serving):

Calories: 313; Fat: 14.48; Carb: 35.98; Protein: 10.87

Air Fryer Pretzel Crescent Rolls

Prep Time: 5 Mins   Total Time: 5 Mins   Serves: 8

Ingredients:

- 1 quart water
- ¼ cup baking soda
- 1 (8 ounce) package refrigerated crescent roll dough
- pretzel salt
- cooking spray

Directions:

1. Place a large stock pot over high heat. Add water and bring to a boil over high heat.
2. Meanwhile shape crescents into desired shape.
3. Heat an air fryer oven to 350 degrees F. Line the air fryer oven with a fitted piece of parchment. Generously spray with cooking spray.
4. Once water is boiling, carefully add baking soda (it WILL bubble up!). Lower crescent rolls into the brine with a spider strainer; boil for 5 seconds. Transfer onto the parchment paper in the air fryer oven. Sprinkle

with salt.

5. Air fry until crescent rolls are cooked through and golden, about 12 minutes. Serve immediately.

Nutritional Value (Amount per Serving):

Calories: 15; Fat: 0.2; Carb: 2.66; Protein: 0.52

Air Fryer Loaded Mashed Potato Cakes

Prep Time: 10 Mins   Cook Time: 12 Mins   Serves: 6

Ingredients:

- 2 cups cold mashed potatoes
- 1 cup shredded Cheddar cheese
- 3 green onions, chopped
- ¼ cup real bacon bits
- 2 tablespoons all-purpose flour
- 1 small egg, beaten

Directions:

1. Combine mashed potatoes, Cheddar cheese, green onions, bacon bits, and flour in a bowl; stir until combined. Mix in beaten egg.
2. Heat air fryer oven to 400 degrees F for 10 minutes.
3. Form mixture into 6 patties and set on a baking sheet. Place baking sheet in the freezer for 10 minutes while you preheat the air fryer oven.
4. Place patties in the air fryer oven in batches, making sure to not overcrowd. Cook undisturbed for 12 minutes. Repeat with remaining patties.

Nutritional Value (Amount per Serving):

Calories: 95; Fat: 2.36; Carb: 14.51; Protein: 4.38

Air Fryer Mini Croissants with Nutella and Jam

Prep Time: 15 Mins   Cook Time: 14 Mins   Serves: 8

Ingredients:

- 1 sheet frozen puff pastry, thawed
- 1 large egg
- 1 tablespoon water
- 8 teaspoons chocolate-hazelnut spread
- 4 teaspoons strawberry jam
- 1 teaspoon cinnamon sugar, or as needed

Directions:

1. Heat air fryer oven to 300 degrees F.
2. Roll out puff pastry on a lightly floured surface into a large square, about 12 inches. Cut into 4 equal squares, and then cut each square in half

diagonally, making 8 triangles.

3. Position the triangle so the wide end is facing you, and the point is away from you. Dip your finger tip in some water, and moisten the edges of each triangle. Whisk the egg and tablespoon of water in a small bowl, and set aside.

4. Add about 1 teaspoon Nutella to the center, and top with about 1/2 teaspoon strawberry jam. Starting on the wide end, roll up dough over the filling toward the point, pinching in the dough, so the filling doesn't ooze out, and shaping the ends into a crescent shape. Brush each crescent with egg wash and sprinkle with cinnamon sugar.

5. Line a baking tray with a parchment liner or spray with cooking spray. Place the croissants into your air fryer oven, seam side down, so they're not touching.

6. Cook in the air fryer oven until golden brown, 11 to 14 minutes. Your cooking time may vary depending on the size and brand of your air fryer oven.

7. Transfer to a wire rack and cool for 5 minutes. Serve warm.

Nutritional Value (Amount per Serving):

Calories: 99; Fat: 5.94; Carb: 10.09; Protein: 1.38

Air Fryer Cherry Cream Cheese Croissants

Prep Time: 10 Mins   Cook Time: 5 Mins   Serves: 8

Ingredients:

- flour for dusting
- 1 (8 ounce) package refrigerated crescent roll dough
- 1 (8 ounce) tub cream cheese
- 1 (15 ounce) can pitted sour cherries, drained
- cooking spray
- ground cinnamon to taste

Directions:

1. Lightly dust a work surface with flour. Unroll crescent dough and divide into triangles along the perforated lines.

2. Spread each triangle with cream cheese.

3. Drop 3 or 4 cherries on the wider portion of each crescent dough triangle. Carefully roll up each crescent, making sure the cherries stay tucked in. Fold down the ends of each roll slightly so it forms a crescent shape.

4. Spray a baking sheet with nonstick cooking spray. Carefully set the croissants into the oven.

5. Set air fryer oven to 400 degrees F.

6. Air fry croissants until puffed up and lightly browned, about 5 minutes. Check to make sure croissants are not sticking to each other and that they are not overly browned. Continue cooking for 2 to 3 minutes longer, making sure they do not get too done.
7. Transfer croissants to a plate and sprinkle with cinnamon.

Nutritional Value (Amount per Serving):

Calories: 123; Fat: 8.38; Carb: 9.91; Protein: 3.08

Air Fryer Grilled Peaches with Cinnamon

Prep Time: 5 Mins   Cook Time: 12 Mins   Serves: 2

Ingredients:

- 1 medium firm peach, halved and pitted
- 2 tablespoons unsalted butter
- 1 teaspoon light brown sugar
- ¼ teaspoon ground cinnamon
- 2 scoops vanilla ice cream

Directions:

1. Heat air fryer oven to 350 degrees F.
2. Place peach halves flesh side down in a baking tray. Cook for 6 minutes.
3. Meanwhile melt butter. Stir in brown sugar and cinnamon until sugar has dissolved.
4. Using tongs, flip peaches over so that they are flesh side up. Brush butter mixture over the top, filling the pit cavity with any excess. Cook for 6 more minutes.
5. Let peaches cool for 5 minutes. Top each half with a scoop of ice cream. Serve immediately.

Nutritional Value (Amount per Serving):

Calories: 123; Fat: 8.4; Carb: 11.94; Protein: 1.69

Sugar Free Yoghurt Scones Air Fryer

Prep Time: 15 Mins   Cook Time: 15 Mins   Serves: 9

Ingredients:

- 2 cups flour
- 1/4 tsp baking powder
- Pinch salt
- Tsp sugar free icing sugar
- Handful raisins
- 30 g cubed butter
- 2 tbsp natural yoghurt
- Tsp vanilla extract

Directions:

1. Put all dry ingredients into a bowl, add butter and vanilla extract and rub in, then make a well to add the yoghurt. Mix to form a soft dough, if wet add more flour.
2. Form a ball.
3. I used a rectangle tin, oiled it lightly, and rolled the dough and pressed it gently into tin.
4. Bake 10 minutes on one side and 5 minutes on the other. At 347°F in air fryer oven.
5. Slice them into squares.

Nutritional Value (Amount per Serving):

Calories: 131; Fat: 3.09; Carb: 21.47; Protein: 3.67

Air Fryer Donuts Recipe

Prep Time: 20 Mins   Cook Time: 5 Mins   Serves: 8

Ingredients:

- ¾ cup granulated sugar
- 2 teaspoons ground cinnamon
- ¼ teaspoon ground nutmeg
- 12 ounces refrigerated jumbo biscuits
- 4 tablespoons salted butter

Directions:

1. In a large shallow bowl, whisk the sugar, cinnamon, and nutmeg together. Set aside.
2. Heat air fryer oven to 350°F.
3. Separate the biscuit dough into individual biscuits and place them onto a clean work surface. Roll each biscuit out to 1-inch thick. Use a biscuit cutter or donut cutter to cut a 1-inch hole out of the center of each biscuit.
4. Spray a baking sheet with nonstick spray.
5. Place the biscuit donuts in a single layer, with space between each, in the air fryer oven. If there isn't room for all of the donuts, cook them in batches.
6. Cook the donuts for 4-5 minutes, or until golden brown all over.
7. While the donuts cook, place the butter into a shallow microwave-safe bowl. Microwave in 30-second increments until melted.
8. Remove the donuts from the air fryer. Immediately dip each donut (both sides) into the melted butter and coat completely with the cinnamon sugar mixture. Serve warm.

Nutritional Value (Amount per Serving):

Calories: 210; Fat: 8.62; Carb: 30.78; Protein: 2.96

Super Easy Air Fryer S'mores

Prep Time: 5 Mins   Cook Time: 5 Mins   Serves: 2

Ingredients:

- 2 Graham Crackers broken in half
- 2 marshmallows broken in half
- 2 small pieces of chocolate

Directions:

1. Place Graham cracker halves in Air fryer oven.
2. Take sticky side of broken marshmallow and place it on the Graham Cracker, pushing down a little so it sticks to the cracker.
3. Close Air Fryer oven and cook on 390 degrees Fahrenheit for 5-7 minutes, or until the tops of the marshmallows are a nice golden color.
4. Once done, add a piece of chocolate on top of the marshmallows, followed by the other half of the graham cracker. Enjoy :)

Nutritional Value (Amount per Serving):

Calories: 85; Fat: 1.73; Carb: 16.15; Protein: 1.26

Copycat Domino's Cinnamon Bread Twists

Prep Time: 15 Mins   Cook Time: 15 Mins   Serves: 6

Ingredients:

- For the Bread Twists Dough
- 1 C All Purpose Flour
- 1 tsp Baking Powder
- 1/4 tsp Kosher Salt
- 2/3 C Fat Free Greek Yogurt
- For Brushing on the Cooked Bread Twists
- 2 Tbsp Light Butter
- 2 Tbsp Granulated Sugar
- 1-2 tsp Ground Cinnamon, to taste

Directions:

1. Mix the flour, baking powder, and salt together before adding the Greek yogurt. Use a fork to stir everything together until a crumbly dough begins to form. Some dry flour should remain in the bowl.
2. Transfer the crumbly dough onto a flat surface and work the dough into one smooth ball of dough. Portion the dough into six 45-gram pieces. Roll the pieces of dough between your palms or on the flat surface to form thin strips, about 8" long.
3. Fold one end of each strip over to form a ribbon shape, and transfer to an air fryer oven baking sheet sprayed with cooking spray. Once all six bread twists are in the oven, spray the top with cooking spray and close the lid.
4. Air fry at 350°F for 15 minutes. (Or bake at 375°F for 25-30 minutes)
5. Towards the end of cooking, microwave the light butter and mix in the

granulated sugar and cinnamon. Brush the cinnamon sugar butter on top of the bread twists as soon as they come out of the air fryer. Serve warm.

Nutritional Value (Amount per Serving):

Calories: 160; Fat: 3.02; Carb: 29.59; Protein: 3.7

Air Fryer Apple Hand Pies

Prep Time: 8 Mins   Cook Time: 10 Mins   Serves: 6

Ingredients:

- 14.1 ounce refrigerated package pie crust (2 crusts)
- 1/2 can (21 ounce) apple pie filling
- 1 large egg
- water
- 3 teaspoons turbinado sugar
- Caramel sauce for dipping, optional

Directions:

1. Remove pie crusts from packaging and allow to come to room temperature, per package instructions.
2. Cut the pie crusts into 5-inch circles using a cookie cutter.
3. Place two slices of apples from the apple pie filling onto the pie crusts on the bottom half of the crust. With a little water on the tip of your finger, moisten the outside edges of the pie crust. Fold dough over filling to form half-moons; pinch the edges of the crust together, then crimp edges with a fork to seal.
4. In a small bowl, whisk together the egg with a splash of water. Brush the pies with the egg wash all over the tops.
5. Sprinkle ½ teaspoon of the coarse sugar over each pie.
6. Make three slits in the crust on the top of the pies.
7. Heat the air fryer oven at 350 degrees F for 5 minutes. Spray a air fryer oven baking tray with nonstick cooking spray.
8. Place 2 pies in the oven at a time, and air fry for about 10 minutes or until the crust is golden brown and filling is bubbling. Carefully remove and transfer to a wire rack to cool. Repeat with remaining pies.
9. Serve with caramel sauce for dipping!

Nutritional Value (Amount per Serving):

Calories: 406; Fat: 19.92; Carb: 54.46; Protein: 2.82

Air Fryer Beignets

Prep Time: 6 Mins   Cook Time: 14 Mins   Serves: 6

Ingredients:

- 1 Cup Self Rising Flour
- 1 Cup Plain Greek Yogurt
- 2 TBSP Sugar
- 1 TSP Vanilla
- 2 TBSP Melted unsalted butter
- 1/2 Cup Powdered Sugar

Directions:

1. Combine the yogurt, sugar & vanilla in a bowl.
2. Add in the flour & stir until it starts to form a dough.
3. Put the dough on to a floured surface.
4. Fold the dough over in half a few times.
5. Shape into a 1"-inch-thick rectangle. Cut it into 9 pieces. Lightly dust each piece with flour.
6. Let them rest for 15 minutes.
7. Preheat your air fryer oven to 350 degrees
8. Spray your air fryer tray with canola spray.
9. Brush the tops of your dough with melted butter.
10. Place butter side down on your tray. Brush the tops of the dough with butter.
11. Air fry for aprx. 6-7 minutes until the edges are starting to brown.
12. Flip over and cook for another 6-7 minutes.
13. Dust with powdered sugar.

Nutritional Value (Amount per Serving):

Calories: 140; Fat: 2.87; Carb: 24.98; Protein: 3.49

Air Fryer Baked Apples

Prep Time: 5 Mins   Cook Time: 15 Mins   Serves: 2

Ingredients:

- 2 Apples
- 1 teaspoon Butter, melted
- ½ teaspoon Cinnamon
- TOPPING INGREDIENTS
- ⅓ cup Old Fashioned / Rolled Oats
- 1 tablespoon Butter, melted
- 1 tablespoon Maple Syrup (or honey or rice malt syrup)
- 1 teaspoon Wholemeal / Whole Wheat Flour, (can sub for almond meal or all purpose flour / plain flour)
- ½ teaspoon Cinnamon

Directions:

Cut apples in half through the stem, and use a knife or a spoon to remove the core, stem and seeds. Brush a teaspoon of butter evenly over the cut sides of the apples, then sprinkle over ½ teaspoon of cinnamon.

Mix topping ingredients together in a small bowl, then spoon on top of the apple halves evenly.

Place the apple halves carefully into the air fryer oven, on a baking sheet, then cook on 350°F for 15 minutes or until softened.

Serve warm with ice cream or cream if desired.

Nutritional Value (Amount per Serving):

Calories: 214; Fat: 6.6; Carb: 44.05; Protein: 3.68

Air Fryer Bread Pudding

Prep Time: 10 Mins   Cook Time: 15 Mins   Serves: 6

Ingredients:

- 2 cups bread cubed
- 1 egg
- 2/3 cup heavy cream
- 1/2 tsp vanilla extract
- 1/4 cup sugar
- 1/4 cup chocolate chips optional

Directions:

1. Spray the inside of a baking dish that fits inside the air fryer oven with cooking spray.
2. Put bread cubes into a baking dish. If using chocolate chips, sprinkle them over the bread.
3. In another bowl, mix the egg, whipped cream, vanilla and sugar.
4. Pour the egg mixture over the bread cubes and let stand for 5 minutes.
5. Put the baking dish inside the air fryer oven. Cook in the air fryer at 350°F for 15 minutes, or until the bread pudding is cooked through.

Nutritional Value (Amount per Serving):

Calories: 133; Fat: 7.72; Carb: 12.78; Protein: 2.98

Air Fryer Berry Hand Pies

Prep Time: 10 Mins   Cook Time: 12 Mins   Serves: 8

Ingredients:

- 1 box store-bought or homemade pie crust
- 1/2 cup berry jam
- 1/2 cup berries
- 1 egg white
- 2 tablespoons coarse sugar
- Optional: Ice cream and additional berries for serving

Directions:

1. Begin by rolling out two pie crusts on a lightly floured surface. Use a 4-inch circle cutter to cut out 14 circles. Ball up the dough scraps. roll out the dough ball, and cut out two more circles.
2. On eight of the 16 circles, place about 2 tablespoons of your jam and top with a bit of fresh fruit.
3. Brush a thin coat of egg white around the edges of the filled circles. Top with the unfilled dough circles and use a fork to crimp the edges. Pierce the top once with a fork to allow the steam to escape during baking.
4. Brush the tops with more of the egg white wash and sprinkle them with caster sugar.
5. Heat the air fryer oven to 375 degrees F. Add four of the prepared pies to the baking tray.
6. Once the air fry is heated, bake the pies about 12 minutes or until the dough is browned.
7. Serve alone or with ice cream and additional fresh berries.

Nutritional Value (Amount per Serving):

Calories: 182; Fat: 6.4; Carb: 28.81; Protein: 2.43

Air Fryer Cheesecake Chimichangas

Prep Time: 10 Mins   Cook Time: 20 Mins   Serves: 8

Ingredients:

- 1 (8 ounce) brick cream cheese, softened to room temperature
- 1/4 cup sour cream, or plain nonfat greek yogurt
- 1½ tablespoons granulated sugar
- 1 teaspoon pure vanilla extract
- 8 medium strawberries, quartered
- 1 medium banana, peeled and sliced
- 8 soft flour tortillas, 8 inches - soft taco size (I use low carb)
- 8 teaspoons nutella
- olive oil spray
- 3 tablespoons melted butter
- 1 recipe cinnamon sugar

Directions:

1. In a medium mixing bowl, cream together the softened cream cheese, sour cream (or greek yogurt), sugar and vanilla until smooth.
2. Divide the cream cheese mixture among 2 medium bowls and toss quartered strawberries in one and sliced bananas in the other. Gently stir to combine (or omit completely).

3. Place a soft flour tortilla on to a clean work surface. Add 1/4 of the strawberry mixture to the left of center on the tortilla. Then add a teaspoon of nutella.
4. Fold the left side of the tortilla over the filling. Fold the short ends in and roll like a burrito.
5. Repeat this with the remaining strawberry mixture, and then do the same with the banana mixture.
6. Spray the chimichangas with olive oil spray and preheat your air fryer oven to 360°. Depending on the size of your air fryer oven, work in batches, placing the chimichangas seam-side down in an even layer, and air frying for 8 to 10 minutes or until the tortilla is a deep golden brown. My air-fryer holds 4 at a time.
7. Once fried, place the chimichangas onto a wire rack set over a rimmed baking sheet. Brushe all sides, nooks and crannies with butter, and then roll in a bowl of cinnamon sugar. Repeat.
8. Prepare to fall in love.

Nutritional Value (Amount per Serving):

Calories: 485; Fat: 29.81; Carb: 35.48; Protein: 19.65

Air Fryer Chocolate Chip Skillet Cookie

Prep Time: 10 Mins   Cook Time: 25 Mins   Serves: 2

Ingredients:

- 1 cup + 2 tablespoons all-purpose flour
- ½ tsp baking soda
- ½ tsp salt
- 6 tbsp butter room temperature
- ⅓ cup granulated sugar
- ¼ cup light brown sugar
- 1 egg
- ½ tsp vanilla extract
- 1 cup semisweet chocolate chips

Directions:

1. Combine the flour, baking soda and salt in a large bowl. Whisk to combine.
2. Add the butter, sugar, brown sugar, egg and vanilla extract and mix well until creamy.
3. Fold in the chocolate chips.
4. Lightly spray a shallow 6 to 7" pie pan with oil.
5. Press the cookie dough into the prepared pan and bake at 340 degrees for 11 minutes.
6. Reduce the heat to 310 degrees and bake another 5 minutes, or until golden brown and cooked through.

Nutritional Value (Amount per Serving):

Calories: 1094; Fat: 66.57; Carb: 121.92; Protein: 15.27

Air Fryer Apple Chips Recipe

Prep Time: 5 Mins   Cook Time: 8 Mins   Serves: 3 cups

Ingredients:

- 3 large sweet, crisp apples, such as Honeycrisp, Fuji, Jazz, or Pink Lady
- 3/4 teaspoon ground cinnamon (optional)
- a pinch of salt

Directions:

1. Start by thoroughly washing your apples. Apples from a farm are usually covered in pesticides. Apples at your grocery store almost always have a waxy coating you need to remove. Either way, don't skip this step!
2. When cutting the apples, you can either core them or you could leave the seeds in the apples. Either way works. Once they are washed and cored, use a mandolin or sharp knife to make rounds that are about 1/8 of an inch thick.
3. Heat your air fryer oven to 390 degrees F. If you are using both cinnamon and salt, mix them in a small bowl. Otherwise, rub the cinnamon into the apple slices and then arrange them on a baking sheet. Place only as many slices that it takes to form a single layer without overlapping the slices.
4. Cook the apple slices for 8 minutes and flip halfway through the cooking time. If they are crisp enough to your liking, you can remove them from the oven and repeat as needed for the remaining apples.
5. If you want them to be crispier, add a small amount of time to the air fryer. We recommend only adding 1 minute at a time until the desired crisp level is reached.

Nutritional Value (Amount per Serving):

Calories: 106; Fat: 0.25; Carb: 27.9; Protein: 1.12

APPENDIX RECIPE INDEX